Can there be such a thing as a deafening whisper?

I saw myself standing atop the Wells Fargo building in downtown Miami overlooking the horizon from the edge of the rooftop. I whispered the words "You either die a hero, or you live long enough to see yourself become the villain". I realized the volume increased with each repetition so I attempted to cover my ears. I began hearing more voices uttering the same phrase so I turned around and saw Brooke, Christian David and a toddler I've never seen. As I took a step towards them, I began to lose my balance and fell off the rooftop just as I jolted awake.

That was definitely interesting. This might have to do something with staying up late, caffeine and having watched The Dark Knight.

I attempt to see the 6:30 a.m. on a bright screen with one eye halfway open. I shine the light just enough to see my bed partner for the night, Christian David, my 3 year old boy, still out. "Man, my back is sore," I thought to myself. Sleeping in a race car bed as your body creates different Tetris shapes is definitely a sacrifice to avoid this little guy from waking Brooke.

I began to inch my way off the bed but of course, this piece of crap creaks. There's a million dollar idea, someone should come up with a kid's bed that will never creak and wake up the kid.

As I make my way downstairs to the kitchen, I hear heavy rain outside. "Oh Miami...you win," I say realizing that my plans to go running this morning have been shattered. As I go for my customary morning Muscle Milk, I glance at the magnetic calendar on the fridge, October 9th. In two weeks, we'll be celebrating our second year in Florida.

Brooke and I decided to move to Florida after I graduated from the University of Utah. As an aspiring newscaster in Miami, I chose to do a full-time news internship for Telemundo with hopes of beginning a lifelong career in media. Meanwhile, I took a job as the evening supervisor at 'Slippery Pete's carwash's Kendall location. Brooke on the other hand has been living her dream. She started as a substitute dance teacher for kids at a studio in Coral Gables. Soon after, she was offered a permanent position at the same studio. She loves it. I love it. She gets to have Christian David with her while she teaches.

As I tilt my head back and try to get every last drop of Muscle Milk, my phone buzzes. It's a reminder for me. Today is the day that I get to drive a brand new Bentley. Unfortunately, it's not for me. "One day baby," I affirm to myself as I throw away the empty Muscle Milk container and plug my phone into a wall charger.

At 9 a.m. I'll be heading downtown to pick up Don Pacho's sweet new ride. Don Pacho is my boss. He owns about 75 Slippery Pete's carwashes across the US and Canada. Like me, he was born in Colombia, but now calls Star Island in Biscayne Bay, home sweet home.

I met Don Pacho at my first summer party here. Slippery Pete's Florida employees put together a summer and Christmas party in Don Pacho's house every year for the past 10 years. I remember when Brooke and I received our party invite and we were so excited, we had to do a quick Google search about all the different celebrity neighbors.

At one point in the party Don Pacho pulled a chair up to our table and introduced himself to us. "I was told that I had to meet the new Colombian supervisor," he said with a heavy accent as he stirred his margarita with a straw. "I heard you're from Bogota, is that right?"

"Yes sir, Juan Camilo Arias Gaviria, para servirle." I answered.

"I don't have good memories of Bogota; it's full of corrupted and egotistic men in politics that don't care about my Colombia." He chuckled.

"I heard you were in politics once many years ago, is that right?" I asked, but all he said was "briefly," as he excused himself from the table to take a call.

In the past year that I've known Don Pacho, I've learned that as a 5'5" unattractive man, with obvious fake blonde hair and way too many plastic surgeries, he lives his life as if he was larger than life. The respect that everyone showers him with everywhere is something you only see with celebrities or nobility. He definitely attracts women as if he was a movie star or a model. It's an amazing thing to see.

I'm sure the hundreds of women I've seen him with are with him because of his personality, not his money. That's how it goes, right?

I did a quick workout, showered and was ready to head out. As I was ordering my Uber ride I could hear Brooke upstairs with Christian David. We're currently on a mission to potty train this kid, but easier said than done.

"Brooke, can I borrow your umbrella?" I yelled. Before she could answer me my phone buzzed. It was a text from the Uber driver, he was already outside. I ran upstairs quickly, kissed my two favorite people and was out the door.

At the dealer, the general manager personally introduced himself to me, and asked me how Don Pacho was enjoying the Rolls Royce Phantom that he purchased a few months back. "I'm sorry I wouldn't know what to tell you, it's my first time picking up a quarter million dollar car for my boss," I said as he signaled me to follow him towards the back of the dealer and explained to me what the protocol was after I left the dealer.

He stopped in front of a new Bentley Continental GT W12. "Man, I need to go into the carwash business," He said as he handed me the key. "Here is the address for MC Customs, Don Pacho will be getting wheels and a full window tint," he added as he handed me a sticky note with his business card.

I could've taken 20th street, and it would've been a straight shot, but I had to let those 600+ ponies loose! I got on the 112 heading west to the car shop and this thing hit 130 mph in a second.

"Hijuemadre....this thing is a beast!" I yelled as I let off the gas a little. I began to contemplate how my life had changed somewhat in the past year.

I was pretty bummed when Telemundo told me that they appreciated my work as an intern, and that I had done wonderfully while there, but unfortunately due to their budget they couldn't offer me a permanent position. Had I chosen the wrong field? Now we were stuck here in Florida.

Once I left Telemundo I was offered the day shift supervising at the carwash. Two weeks into the new hours Don Pacho came in with a matte black Ferrari to have it detailed. He came into the supervisor's office and asked, "Juancho, viste el golazo de James contra Uruguay?" Translation, "did you see James' goal against Uruguay?" Don Pacho was a huge futbol fan like every Colombian, and was following the Colombian national team during the 2014 FIFA World Cup.

"Of course Don Pacho," I answered as I stood up to shake his hand, and turned off the flat screen in the office with post-match commentary. "What brings you around here?"

"I want to celebrate Colombia's win today with some great Colombian food, and I thought I needed to have some Colombian company, so I'm here to take you to a late lunch," he said. Once the Ferrari was detailed, he took me to a Colombian restaurant south of the downtown area. Our late lunch went on for two hours and surprisingly, we talked very little futbol. After we finished eating, he said that he wanted to know more about me and my current situation. I talked about my internship, my family and how things were going for us in our new life in Florida.

Prior to leaving the restaurant, Don Pacho popped his head into the kitchen to thank the staff for the food. Pretty cool gesture, I had never seen anyone do that before.

As we walked over to the parking lot, Don Pacho handed me the car key and asked, "Juancho, have you ever driven a Ferrari?"

My eyes got wide and I could feel the smile creep across my face.

I tightened my grip on the steering wheel as I merged into the off ramp, the sound this thing makes as 12 cylinders downshift is pretty sexy!

The guys at MC Customs took the car in, so I stepped inside the waiting area to call Don Pacho and tell him that I had made it to the car shop. He asked me if I could do one more thing for him before I dropped the car off.

"Of course Don Pacho, anything," I said as I got a pen and a sticky note from the receptionist.

"Can you go by Monserrate Restaurant and pick me up some food; you remember the restaurant we went to that one day?" he asked.

"Yes sir, what would you like?" I asked as I got ready to jot down the items. "They should know my order by now," he chuckled.

When the Bentley was ready, I was told by a staff member that the car had a return appointment for the full body wrap in matte black. "I.....don't know, Don Pacho didn't...," I was interrupted by the manager as he walked into the front office. "Don Pacho has all his cars wrapped in matte black."

"Alright, if you say so..." I responded.

As I pulled up to a red light, I began thinking to myself how I could definitely get used to this, not only working for a wealthy man, but to be the one with the money. I've tried starting a couple of businesses without much success. I've tried several ideas in manufacturing, importing, tech and fashion - but nothing has worked out yet. I recently read a book by

Mark Cuban, a pretty short read that finished with 'You only have to be right once!'

When I made it to the restaurant, the owner took care of me right away. I didn't even have to say a word about the order. In minutes, I was on my way out the door with two bags of fresh Colombian food.

As I entered the Star Island community, the guards didn't even stop me; I guess I looked like a local resident returning from a joy ride in a quarter million dollar toy. As I rolled past the first few set of homes, I remembered the celebrity website I had read about this neighborhood. Shaq was living or had lived here as well as Gloria Estefan, Rosie O'Donnell and Diddy. These mansions were beyond anything I had ever seen back in Utah.

I pulled up to Don Pacho's driveway which seemed more like a small airstrip than a driveway, lined up with imported palm trees and waist high bushes covered in flowers of all colors. As I continued my trek on the airstrip towards the house, I noticed the sound of the new water feature that Don Pacho had installed in front of the house. He was a regular in Las

Vegas, and had mentioned to me how he would love to have a mix of the water fountains from the Bellagio and the river in the Venetian.

I finally made it to the house, or "Palazzo Napoli" as Don Pacho called it. He had renovated the whole place. He tore down the Scarface mansion and turned Tony Montana's compound into a Tuscan style mansion.

With money anything is possible.

"Door number four is open," said one of the man servants while pointing towards the 20-car garage in the back. "Geez....door number four out of eight doors for a car garage, just insane," I said to myself as I gave this beauty one last rev.

Brooke and I missed the tour last time we were here, so I didn't get to see the garage. The man had a couple of Rolls Royce's, the new Bentley, a Bugatti Vincero decked out in carbon fiber, three or four Ferrari's, a Gurkha LAPV truck, a Mercedes Benz 6X6 and a Mercedes Benz GL550. Aside from the Mercedes SUV, the car I had picked up today was the cheapest of the group, nothing like having a few million dollars in exotic cars to play with!

I handed the two bags of food to a maid, while another one took me to the back of the house where Don Pacho was on his yacht. "Juancho, how does the car drive?" asked Don Pacho as he sat down to slip on his spiffy blue suede top-siders. "And how does it look with the new wheels?" he shouted as he signaled one of the two girls in bikinis to lower the Vallenato music that was blasting through the yacht's outer speakers.

"Like a car that Tony Montana would drive," I said with a smile.

As he climbed out of the yacht, he made a comment on how he wanted to rename the yacht, and encouraged me to think of one. In fact, he said that he was offering $2,000 to the best name that anyone, including his staff, came up with and was chosen as the winner.

After a brief chat and dinner with the boss, I pulled out my phone to order an Uber ride, but Don Pacho stopped me. He made a comment about how Brooke and I needed a second car. To this day, we had been sharing a

Toyota Corolla and it was tough. Putting in and taking out a toddler car seat was such a pain.

Don Pacho had me follow him to the side of the house, where his staff had parked the Mercedes Benz GL550 I saw in the garage. "I know it's a couple of weeks early, but say *'Happy Birthday'* to Brooke for me," he said as he handed me the keys with a wink.

"Don Pacho….I…um…I uh…?" I was completely speechless. It's not every day that someone gives you a brand new car, let alone a Benz.

"Juancho, you're an exceptional person and employee, but the one thing that I admire the most about you is your family," he said as he smiled and placed a hand on my shoulder. "Family should be the number one thing in a man's life, no matter what!" he added as the smile faded, "I too love my family and would do anything for them, even die for them." Don Pacho always mentioned his family and how much he loved them, but he never mentioned anything about going back to Colombia or having his family visit him here.

"Don Pacho, thank you so much….this is such a blessing for us right now," I said as I shook his hand. I sat in the driver's seat and buckled in. "Go home Juancho, take the rest of the day off….oh and one more thing, you and the family have a dinner reservation tonight at 7:30PM at Nobu, it's a Japanese restaurant in South Beach, they'll be expecting you." he said.

On my way home I got a call from my dad. My dad calls almost every day to ask how we're doing, give me advice and especially ask how his only grandson is doing. Too bad my parents only had me. They could easily have an army of grandchildren at this point in their lives.

I told my dad about how Don Pacho was giving Brooke a new SUV for her birthday and a nice dinner tonight at a high end restaurant. As always my dad voiced his concern, worry, or skepticism, whatever you want to call it, about the true "intentions" of this treatment for the past year. You know that his advice has a subtle warning when he calls me by my first and middle name - Juan Camilo. It was obvious that my dad didn't like Don Pacho for some reason. Oh well, he overthinks things too much.

I wrapped up the call as I was parking in front of our building rather than our underground spot.

About two months ago, our little family had the opportunity of buying a new two story condo on the 7th & 8th floor of the Colonnade community just north of the Dadeland Mall in Kendall. We had been living in a one bedroom one bathroom apartment in Hialeah, and while it was a great place for us, we had outgrown it and felt we wanted a little more for us. We had contemplated moving back to Utah where according to Forbes magazine, the state was rated as one of the top places for business in the United States. I had also been considering getting my MBA; after all I've always wanted to be a businessman. However, we decided to establish ourselves here.

The decision to stay was easier to make after I was promoted to Director of Public Relations for all 75 Slippery Pete's locations, which by the way, came with a substantial pay increase, three times more than what I was making as a supervisor. Since we were on the fence about staying in Florida, we hadn't decided on buying a second car, but things started to come together nicely for us in Florida. I almost forgot to mention that Don Pacho even loaned us a 20% down payment for our place.

In the elevator I tried to think of a clever way to surprise Brooke with the new Mercedes SUV, but I was blank, so I decided to let the car do the talking.

I opened the door as carefully as I could to avoid being heard. I could hear the shower on as I got closer to our bedroom. I kissed my boy Christian David who was on our bed using Brooke's iPad, he was watching some Justice League cartoons, which Brooke does not approve of, but hey, I grew up with that stuff and I turned out alright. I continued into the bathroom like a ninja. I popped my head in on one side of the shower and waited for Brooke to turn around since she was doing a vertical half-split on the wall while shaving her leg. No need for me to scream, as soon as she saw me she let out a high pitch scream that makes it all worth my effort.

"Juan, why are you home early?" asked Brooke.

"Don Pacho told me to go home and get you guys ready to go celebrate your birthday," I responded as I joined the little man on our bed.

"Really!?" she said as she walked out of the bathroom while drying her hair.

"So when are we going to stop walking around naked in front of Christian David?" I asked since she was giving us both a show.

"I don't know. Did your boss really say that?" she added as she wrapped herself in a towel.

"Well, kind of," I chuckled.

"What does that mean?" she asked with a confused look on her face.

"Dress nice princess, we're eating out tonight at a Japanese restaurant that Don Pacho recommended for your birthday," I yelled as I carried Christian David to his room to get him ready.

Once we were out the door and made our way downstairs, I picked up Christian David and opened the back door of the Mercedes. "Juan, what are you doing?" Brooke sounded alarmed.

"Oh, I forgot to mention it upstairs, Don Pacho sent you this as an early birthday present," I answered. She just stared at me without a response. "Did you hear what I said?" I asked.

"He gave you a brand new SUV!?" she asked sarcastically.

"I am completely serious princess," I tried to sound as reassuring and believable as possible.

"Why...who...who gives a new car?" still sounding doubtful.

"Hey, I stopped wondering THAT when he gave me the raise, when he gave us the down payment and when he took me to the Champions League Final in Berlin." I quickly added.

Don Pacho and I took his private jet on a direct flight to Berlin this past June to watch the Champions League Final between Barcelona and Juventus. Without a doubt an unbelievable experience that is only second to the birth of Christian David and our wedding day. To top it off, Don Pacho has some contacts in the Barcelona organization and we had the opportunity to meet Lionel Messi, Neymar and Luis Suarez before the match. Can it get better than that?

Since it was Brooke's new car, she got to hop behind the wheel and drive us to Nobu.

It's amazing how Don Pacho got this SUV right. I had made a brief comment months ago about how I wanted to get Brooke a sky blue GL with full tint, this and that, but never did I think that he would do this for us. During the drive I was going through the glovebox compartment and I found another little surprise from the world's greatest.

An envelope addressed to Familia Arias, inside a short note with a large silver key, and a large gold key. The note said the following, 'Juancho, Brooke and Christian David, family is the most important thing in life, and that's why you'll be taking my jet tomorrow and heading to California. You'll be staying for a week in my Laguna Beach house (silver key). Below is the contact information for one of my drivers that will be waiting for you. Just call him and let him know once you're in the air. Also, I want you to make a stop in Utah and do two things for me. First, get both sets of parents. They'll be going with you on the trip. Second, I need you Juancho to do me a favor and stop by my Park City house (gold key). My Utah driver will pick you up at the airport, and will also be available to take you up to the house in Park City. Call me once you're at the house so I can give you further instruction. Enjoy your trip. Un abrazo, Don Pacho."

I think I'm living in a modern day fairy tale.

After dinner, the restaurant manager came to our table to ask how we had enjoyed our dinner. "I hope that you still have room for dessert," he said as he directed our waiter to display two different kinds of desserts, "Don Pacho always enjoys our Guru Berii and Harumaki. He suggested that you try them both."

"Thank you, they both look amazing," Brooke said as she intercepted Christian David's wondering hand from going for the Harumaki.

I decided to go for the Guru Berii but Brooke stopped me before I could take a bite. "Before we have dessert, I want to show you a picture that Christian and I took earlier today at Costco, I think we found his Halloween costume," she said as she handed Christian David a picture, "Can you give that to Daddy!?"

I looked at the picture with Christian David dressed as Batman and holding a smaller Robin costume. "Cool, I love it!" I said being the huge Batman fan that I am. "We got both costumes." added Brooke. "Why did you buy both?" I asked, "The Robin one looks like it's for a baby."

"It is." Brooke said with a smile and a twinkle in her eye.

I realized what she was saying, and before I could say anything Christian David pointed at the Robin costume and said "Baby."

"Oh my....Brooke, are you pregnant?!" I asked in unbelief.

"Yup, and it's a boy in case you still can't tell from the picture." she chuckled since we had talked about how we wanted a little girl after Christian David someday in the future.

"Wait, so you already know it's a boy? How long have you known that you were pregnant?" I asked.

"Oh, 17 weeks," she answered, "I was wondering when you were going to notice."

I leaned over the table and gave Brooke a kiss. "I love you, I'm so sorry if I've been in the clouds lately. I'm so glad that we have a third bedroom now!" I said still smiling at the news. La Familia Arias was now going to have four crew members!

Brooke asked me to drive on our way back home. I glanced at the rear view mirror and I could see that Christian David was already out.

"Are you ready for two boys?" whispered Brooke while reaching for my hand.

I smiled as an answer to her question. We were comfortable financially. We had paid off all debt including school loans, had plenty of room for a new addition to the family and were beginning to set aside a good chunk in savings. Life was great.

Once we made it home, I changed Christian David's diaper and put him in bed.

After Brooke came out of the bathroom, I began brushing my teeth in hopes that we could continue the celebration, but she quickly shut me down and said that she wasn't feeling too well and was going straight to bed.

I kissed her good night.

Since I had brushed my teeth for nothing I grabbed a snack and headed to the couch with Brooke's iPad. I finished watching Breaking Bad a week ago on Netflix, and next on my list was NARCOS. Everyone on social media kept raving about it, and I had recently read it was all shot on location, plus I wanted to see a fresh new look on the world's most infamous Colombian and his reign of terror.

In my opinion Escobar wasn't "killed" in 1993. I remember living in Colombia during that time, and even today, a man that had evaded the Colombian and US government, army, DEA, FBI, CIA and everybody else, had gone down so easily with just one other henchman by his side? C'mon, he could easily have escaped, changed his look and be living like a king in South Beach or the south of France for last couple of decades.

I was halfway into the third episode when my phone rang. Who calls at 3am? The caller ID showed it was the boss. "Don Pacho, how can I help you?" I asked.

"Juancho...I need you to go pick up my money," he slurred his words. The man was heavily drunk and I could hear several female voices in the background.

"Don Pacho, what money are you talking about?" I replied. "The money that…." The phone went dead. I tried calling back several times but he didn't answer. Oh well, I guess I'll try again tomorrow morning before heading to the airport. I silenced my phone so I could continue watching my show, but I noticed that the iPad only had 1% power left. Brooke never charges this thing.

I decided to sneak in a couple of games of FIFA on the Xbox before going to bed. I've never been a gamer in fact the only seven games that I own are the same thing since 2009.

After restarting the last game a few times due to getting scored on first, I decided to call it a night.

I had barely turned off the light when I heard footsteps behind the couch. It was Christian David; the poor guy has night-terrors just like his mom. I picked him up and headed for his room, but he asked for a drink of water, or Wa Wee as he calls it.

SATURDAY OCTOBER 10TH, 2015

After a "restful" five hours of sleep in a mini race car, we decided to get up and get ready for our trip. Brooke had already been up packing for a while. "Good morning princess," I said with a yawn.

"Goooood morning!" she answered cheerfully.

"Somebody is in a good mood." I replied. "I'm guessing that you're feeling better this morning?" I added.

"Definitely!" she mumbled as she took a bite of a bagel with cream cheese.

"Can you get Christian ready while I finish up packing?" she asked.

"Sure, but first I need to make a quick phone call to Don Pacho. He called me last night." I said.

I stepped out to our balcony to make the call. While the phone was ringing I noticed that on the opposite building across the street, about the same floor level, there was a guy in a white shirt and tie looking at me through some kind of telescope. He wasn't out on the balcony but rather inside the condo with the sliding door open pointing this thing at me. He must have been looking at me, because as soon as we made eye contact he walked away.

"Good morning, Palazzo Napoli, how can I help you?" asked one of Don Pacho's maids. They really answered the phone like that.

"Good morning, Don Pacho por favor," I asked as I glanced over at our peeping Tom across the street.

"Juancho, are you flying already?" murmured Don Pacho. The guy must have the biggest hangover.

"Not yet Don Pacho, I was returning your call from last night," I answered.

"Last night?" he sounded confused.

"Yes sir, you said something about wanting me to pick up some money for you, but then we got disconnected and I couldn't get through anymore." I replied.

"Oh Ok, yes I have a little assignment for you for when you get back from your vacation. Do you have a Colombian or US passport?" he asked.

"US, I just got it. I took and passed the US Citizenship test last summer and it took me a while to get the US Passport process started." I answered as I glanced one more time over at my nosey neighbor in the other building. The sliding door was now shut, as well as the blinds.

"Alright, well, we'll talk more about it when you come back. For now, I'll expect a call from you once you're at my house in Park City." he added.

The call ended and we finished getting ready and made it to the airport and the plane took off around noon.

Once we landed at Salt Lake International airport, Don Pacho's driver picked us up and took us to Brooke's family's house in Draper for the night. Brooke must have done the check-in thing on Facebook, because I started getting texts from a couple of different people including my cousin who wanted me to play some futsal at Soccer City tonight. I replied back and said that I totally would love to, luckily I had packed my indoor soccer shoes, but I would need a ride.

After joining my parents for dinner at Café Rio, we solidified the plans for the following day. I would head up to Park City in the morning; do whatever I needed to do, and around 5 p.m. we would all meet at the airport. After dinner Brooke and my mom said they wanted some ice cream next door at Cold Stone, there's nothing better than giving sugar to your 3-year-old right before bed time.

My freezing Utah night ended with some futsal with my cousin and a toddler that would not go to sleep.

SUNDAY OCTOBER 11TH, 2015 – DRAPER, UT

After another night of minimal sleep, I got ready and was about to leave when Brooke asked if she could tag along with her mom and sister. They wanted to go shopping at the Outlet stores in Park City while I did my thing.

After dropping them off, my driver drove me to the house, which looked more like a ski resort than a house. The place was massive, 23-thousand square foot of mansion atop of a hill overseeing Jordanelle Reservoir to the east and Downtown Park City to the west. The name engraved on the enormous steel gate doors fit the property well, La Catedral.

Once I was inside the house I called Don Pacho. "Go to the master bedroom on the second floor it's the last door at the end of the south wing of the house. Behind the winter coats in the closet you will see a green button, press it," he instructed me as I made my way up the stairs and down the hall.

Like out of a movie, once I pressed the button the island in this walk-in closet opened up. Instead of seeing expensive watches and jewelry, the whole thing was a built in safe. "You'll need the password to open it. It's MiTata61," he directed me.

I could see some stacks of cash, a couple Rolexes, what looked like a samurai sword, some thick leather binders and a gold 9mm hand gun.

"It's open Don Pacho," I said.

"I need you to take both binders with you Juancho and leave them in the jet for the week," he ordered, "and make sure that you hear two clicks once you close the safe."

"It's done." I confirmed.

"Alright Juancho, thank you for doing this for me, see you in a week," he said.

On our way back home, we stopped at the Cheesecake Factory for a quick lunch. I decided to call my parents to tell them I had ordered a limo service to pick them up. "Papa, don't worry, it wasn't expensive. Just be ready at 3:00 p.m. A black town car will be picking you both up," I said.

At my in-law's house, our driver was able to pack all seven of us into the black Escalade. I forgot to mention my brother-in-law and sister-in-law had also joined our California bound party. So Brooke's family and my parents brought the head count to nine people. Not too bad. Don Pacho said that this house had 14 or 15 bedrooms with just as many bathrooms.

I'll know I made it when I forget how many bedrooms one of my many mansions has.

Once in route to John Wayne airport in Santa Ana, I made a quick call to notify Don Pacho's driver about our arrival.

"So what's in the binders?" asked my mom.

"No clue, he didn't say." I answered.

"They look expensive," said Brooke, "Can you take a peek?"

"Even if I wanted to, I can't. They have a code locking system." I said.

"Ladies and Gentlemen, we'll be arriving at John Wayne airport in 20 minutes," the pilot interrupted over the speaker system.

"Can I get anyone else anything before landing?" asked our flight attendant. Don Pacho liked traveling with someone to take care of his every need. The jet had some snacks, drinks, and even a couple of wine bottles.

After landing we packed our bags into a Mercedes Benz Sprinter and made the short 25 minute drive to the house in Laguna Beach.

Every house owned by Don Pacho that I've been to so far is nothing short of a masterpiece. This one in Irvine Cove even has access to its own private beach.

By the time we arrived, the sun was just about to set so we decided to leave the beach for the next day. We did however enjoy an amazing sunset in the infinity pool while Don Pacho's personal chef and crew prepared dinner for us.

MONDAY OCTOBER 12TH, 2015 – LAGUNA BEACH, CA

The following morning before anyone was up I got in a quick workout in the home gym. By the time everyone was up, the kitchen crew had set up a breakfast buffet for us.

"Juan, I want to go to the beach, can you please find our boy and change him into his swim shorts?" my sweet wife asked. "The water diapers and spray on sunscreen are in the outside pocket of Christian's bag."

The kid had bolted without us noticing and had gone exploring around the house. It took me a good five minutes to find him. He had made his way to a large office on the second floor. "Christian David, you shouldn't be in here by yourself buddy," I said as I glanced at a wall covered in magazine and newspaper cutouts.

As I focused on a few, I noticed the whole wall was an enormous collage of Pablo Escobar. The majority of the pictures and cutouts were about his death in the early 90s, but a few were about when he ran for the Colombian Congress, when he was named 'El Robin Hood Paisa' by the media and the first Forbes article that included him as one of the richest men in the world.

"Wow, I think Don Pacho has a man crush on Escobar." I said as I picked up Christian David and closed the door behind us.

The rest of the day consisted of playing on the beach, eating another stellar lunch prepared by the staff and the Lakers home opener in a private suite. I had received a call from someone at the Staples Center earlier in the day giving us the options of food for that night.

Our week here went by pretty quickly. Each day was pretty much the same. Brooke and I had a date night in midweek. Our driver took us in Don Pacho's Rolls Royce to a performance of Lord of the Dance in downtown LA. This was our second time watching this show. The first one had been for our first Valentine's Day as a married couple in Utah at Kingsbury Hall.

MONDAY OCTOBER 19TH, 2015 – MIAMI, FL

In a blink of an eye we were back in Florida. We had dropped off both families in Utah, except my sister-in-law who had asked if she could stay with us until the end of November when we returned to Utah for Thanksgiving.

This morning, I woke up at 8:30 a.m. with plans to make it in to the office at 10 a.m. The only appointment I have set up for today is at 1 p.m. with the Dade County School District. We're considering being the title sponsor for the Young Entrepreneurs Give Back program. The program encourages students of any age to come up with a business idea that will also give back to the community. If we move forward with this sponsorship, Slippery Pete's will be providing the award money for the finalists. Don Pacho has made it clear to me that my main focus should be giving back to the community and strengthening our local presence in all of our locations.

I was putting my tie on when I heard a knock on the door.

"Buenos dias Don Pacho, I was going to call you in a few minutes about what you wanted me to do with the binders," I said.

"Tranquilo Juancho, I was in the area and I thought I might as well drop in to discuss a couple of things with you," he said.

What threw me off was that I had never shared with Don Pacho the exact building or number of our condo. Plus, I still haven't updated my home address in our system back at work.

"Can I get you anything Don Pacho?" I asked from the kitchen. "Do you have any beer?" he asked me as he pulled a chair at our dining table. "Sorry Sir, we don't drink. I have some Pony Malta if you'd like?" I quickly added.

"Sure," he replied, "Where is the family?"

"Brooke, Christian David and my sister-in-law left early this morning to run an errand before her dance classes," I answered.

I began looking for the bottle opener but couldn't find it. I remembered seeing Christian David playing with it in his room. "Don Pacho, I'll be right back. My kid has the bottle opener in his room," I said as I ran up the stairs.

The little man's room was a mess but luckily I could see the bottle opener on his dresser. Before I stepped out of the room I opened the blinds and let some light in. While doing so, I looked across towards my nosey neighbor from across the street, and there he was again pointing his telescope towards my place. "What is up with this guy?" I shouted to myself as I left the room.

"Sorry for the wait Don Pacho," I apologized on my way down the stairs. "I just don't know what to do about my neighbor."

"Neighbor?" he asked.

"Yeah, my neighbor from across the street, I've caught him a few times looking or spying on us with his telescope," I said while taking the cap off of his Pony Malta.

"In fact, he's looking at us right now. It's the condo across the street on the same floor," I explained.

What happened next is straight out of a sitcom or movie. Without a word Don Pacho stood up, stepped out to the balcony, took out a Cuban cigar, took a puff, glanced at my neighbor, flipped him off, came back inside, shut the sliding door and sat back down, still not a word.

"Thank you Sir?" I said sounding unsure of my gratitude.

"Don't thank me yet Juancho," he said as he pulled out a little black pocket book and wrote something in it. "I've dealt with people like that in the past and they eventually learn that if you play with fire you get burned."

"Alright, now for the reason I was here," he said while opening one of the two leather binders. "This whole binder contains very important business information," he paused and signaled me to move closer to him, "that I feel is necessary for you to know."

The binder was divided in two sections, businesses and investments. The first section was organized with color coded tabs that corresponded to a certain industry. I flipped through a few of the pages and I saw companies in the frozen poultry industry, telecommunications, apparel, fruit, hospitality, entertainment, transportation and many more. Don Pacho owned all of these 100%.

The second section of the binder was even more impressive. It was also color coded. It listed his prior investments in different industries as well. What surprised me the most of this section was reading the names of well-known companies and corporations worldwide where he had invested different amounts of money. I saw popular tech companies in social media, including major apps, sports companies, retail stores, sports drinks, oil companies, real estate, film studios, casinos and even professional sports teams in almost every sport.

My mind was completely blown. I was under the impression that I was employed by a multimillionaire who owned 75 locations of Slippery Pete's carwashes across the US and Canada. Not so, this man was a multibillionaire with his money sprinkled all over the world. How was this guy not on the Forbes 400?

"Juancho, I think it's time for another promotion," he chuckled. "You will now be the VP of Marketing & Public Relations for all of my business ventures. The job will require some traveling domestically and internationally," he explained as he opened his little handbook and tore a piece of paper. "But it won't be excessive as to keep you away from your family. In fact, you can take them along on some of the trips if you want," he added and handed me the blank piece of paper.

"Here...," he said while giving me his pen. "Write the amount of money that you want to be paid for this new job."

"Don Pacho, are you serious?" I asked in disbelief. "Don't get me wrong, thank you so much for the promotion, I gladly accept it. But are you serious about my pay?"

"Juancho, I think you've worked with me enough time to know when I'm joking and when I'm serious," he said as he took a puff of his cigar. "Write a number!" he repeated.

In my previous pay raise Don Pacho had tripled my salary to a six figure annual income. I had been making $40,000 as a full time supervisor, and just like that I was making enough to buy a condo and pay off everything we owed leaving us with zero debt.

I conservatively increased my current salary by ten percent, but to my amazement he asked me to try again. This time I added 25% but he simply scratched it off. I added 30%, scratched it off again. 40% 50% 60% 70%, nothing, he just scratched off all of them.

"Don Pacho, I don't understand," I said. "What am I supposed to write?"

"Juancho, I want you to write a number that you want as your new annual salary. Give me an amount that you believe is fair for this amount of responsibility." He replied.

I doubled my current pay to $240,000 a year. As if it was a joke, he scratched it off once again and said, "Closer, but try one more time." I didn't know what to do. I've never heard of this happening to anyone, even in movies. Is he really serious? Does he want me to write a bigger amount?

Alright, here you go.

$500,000

I handed the piece of paper back to him. He stared at the number for what seemed like an eternity.

He stood up, took one last sip of his Pony Malta, slid the paper towards me and asked for the pen.

He added a zero. He ADDED a zero!

"Don Pacho, that's $5 million." I emphasized. "That is $5 million, I'm glad you know your numbers Juancho." He replied sarcastically.

"Don Pacho, you're going to pay me 5 million dollars...a year?" I asked. "Who do I need to kill?"

"No one yet," he said with a wink and a smile.

I've always heard that when people experience a near death situation their whole life plays before them. Obviously this scenario wasn't anything like that but I did have many thoughts and flashes go through my mind in a matter of seconds. My thoughts were mainly 'Can this really happen to someone?' and 'It's too good to be true'.

My Father and his dislike of Don Pacho come to mind, and I can only imagine what he'll say as soon as he knows about this 'promotion'.

I must have been in deep thought for some time. "Juancho, do you have good reception up there?" he joked. "Is that going to be a satisfactory amount for your services?" he quickly asked before I said anything.

"Do things like this happen in this world?" I asked as I stared at the number.

"They do in my world Juancho," he nodded with conviction.

"Well, I'm glad I'm being introduced to your world Don Pacho," I nodded and smiled. "You're changing my family's life."

"I'm happy to be that person. Just know that even better things are coming your way my friend." He said.

Once we wrapped up, Don Pacho mentioned how he would introduce the second binder to me tomorrow. He wanted me to join him at an open house for the new Brabus USA office in Miami.

"Juancho, I'll pick you up at the office at 1:45 p.m. and we'll head over together," he said.

He thanked me for my time, told me that I would be given a copy of the information from the first binder and excused himself.

I headed upstairs to finish putting on my tie since I was struggling with my concentration. I think it had to do with the fact that I had been made a millionaire just a few moments ago. After a few attempts and a few bursts of random laughter, I too was out the door.

The rest of the day went smoothly. I was definitely in a great mood. I had my meeting with the Dade County School District and we agreed the terms of the title sponsorship. Slippery Pete's would contribute a total of $25,000 for the winner, $10,000 for the runner up and $5,000 for third place.

At the end of the day, I tried to beat the traffic by leaving a few minutes before 5 p.m., but that was just wishful thinking. Traffic was bumper to bumper so I had plenty of time to think of a way to surprise my princess with the news of the day. I decided to call home and let Brooke know that traffic was slower than usual for a Monday and it could take a while for me to get home.

While the phone rang, I thought of buying a pizza on my way home and writing $5 million on the inside of the box under the pizza. The call went to voicemail. I waited a couple of minutes and tried again, but voicemail again. Traffic was horrible so I decided to get off and just take the streets.

I stopped at our favorite pizza joint, Anthony's Coal Fired Pizza, which is only about a 7 minute drive from our place. But before I stepped out of the car, I thought I might try calling Brooke again to tell her to not make dinner. This time she answered immediately.

"Juan, there's a fire across the street in the other building!" she sounded alarmed, "Where are you?"

"I stopped to get a couple of pizzas at Anthony's but never mind, I'm on my way," I answered as my heart began to race. I quickly started the car and rushed back home.

As I got closer to our street I could see and smell the smoke. The entrance to our underground parking was blocked by one of the fire trucks forcing me to park around the corner.

When I made it in, Brooke and Christian David were attentively watching the firefighters from the balcony.

"Where's the fire?" I asked.

"They already put it out, but it was in that condo." She said pointing at a 7th floor condo from across the street. Brooke was pointing at none other than the condo with the nosey neighbor with the telescope.

"Oh man, that's the condo I was telling you about the other day, the one with the telescope." I said.

"I counted five body bags," she said, "At least they contained it from spreading to the other condos, it could've been so much worse."

"Honey, I'm sorry, with all this I didn't get to make dinner," she added.

"Don't worry princess, I was thinking about getting a couple of pizzas anyway," I said while getting my phone out to place the order. "Where's your sister?"

"She's at the gym downstairs," Brooke answered.

Anthony's took my order and told me that it would be a 45 minute wait. I took that time to rethink of a way to tell Brooke the great news from this morning. I wouldn't be able to use the pizza anymore.

While waiting, I decided to step out to our balcony and join Brooke, Christian David and all our neighbors as different groups scrambled to get the scene under control down below. Christian David loved picking out all the different vehicles. The street was covered with fire fighters, police cars, ambulances and a couple of black SUVs.

"Who's that?" I asked about the black SUV's.

"I don't know, it was a bunch of guys with ties," answered Brooke as she took Christian David inside. "Alright mister, I think we've had enough of the fire, time for a bath."

After Christian David's bath, I turned on the TV in the living room to catch the last few minutes of Shark Tank but someone was at the door. Plus I was too late the 9 p.m. news was starting.

"Pizza is here," I shouted in excitement.

"It'll be $24.88," said the surfer dude with my pizzas.

"Brooke, can you bring me a $10 dollar bill please?" I shouted towards the kitchen.

'Next on 7News, a developing story coming out of Kendall where a high-rise condo fire has been contained but has claimed the lives of several people reports say...'

"Hey Brooke, 7News is doing a live shot across the street about the fire!" I shouted over the TV.

"I've delivered tons of pizzas to that condo before," said the pizza delivery guy, "I think they were FBI or DEA guys."

"FBI or DEA, are you serious?" I asked.

"Yeah, their walls were covered in maps and I think I saw a bullet proof vest with DEA on it once," he answered.

FBI, DEA? Why was the FBI or DEA spying on us? Why were they surveilling us?

I paid the kid and closed the door still trying to get my thoughts straight.

"Juan, are you ok?" asked Brooke.

"Ah yeah," I said, "Let's eat."

"What's wrong?" she insisted.

"Nothing princess, I was just wondering if I got the right change," I answered.

After our late dinner, Brooke headed upstairs to put the little guy to bed. I stepped out to the balcony again. The last thing on my mind was sleep. I stayed up late thinking of any reason why I would be under surveillance. This had to be a mistake. I've never done anything illegal in my life.

I didn't know what to think. Why in the world would the FBI or DEA be checking us?

I stared at the burnt condo and I had a series of thoughts come to me. Don Pacho, my out of this world promotion, Don Pacho flipping off these guys, his little black notebook and whatever he wrote in it. Could Don Pacho be involved in this? I suddenly remembered his comment about how you get burned when you play with fire. Don Pacho did this. But why, why would Don Pacho do this? This doesn't make sense!

One thing was sure, I can't tell Brooke about my promotion, at least not yet. Brooke would just worry too much, to the point of physically and emotionally affecting her, stress that an expecting mother doesn't need. Plus I need to make sure that we're not in any kind of danger before I know how to proceed. Maybe all of this happens to be an amazing case of coincidence.

I will have to open a separate bank account and continue to deposit the same amount of money into our joint account before the first deposit of 200K is made.

But what if he DID do it? Should I mess around with a guy like that?

It was starting to get a little cold outside so I decided to go to the couch to try to get my mind off of all this. I pulled out my phone to watch the rest of the third episode of NARCOS that I couldn't finish a week ago.

I don't think I stayed awake long because the next thing I remember is having a really weird sequential dream. I was standing alone in front of my old Communication Law classroom at the University of Utah. I was speaking to an empty room about who I was and what my plans were, only I never mentioned what those plans were or for what purpose. Next I heard a voice behind me asking me to please sit down. As I took my seat I noticed that the room was now full of men in suits and ties but we were no longer in my old classroom. I was now in a large room that looked like the Congress room at the Capitol. The room was surrounded by flags from all over the world with the Colombian flag right in the middle behind a panel of men staring at me.

One of these men asked me to please be quiet and leave the room. As I stood up I suddenly realized that I was now looking at myself from a third person view and I wasn't myself, I was Don Pacho, or had been Don Pacho all along. I proceeded to walk out of the room but stopped myself before leaving the building. I then pulled out Don Pacho's little black book and wrote the word "Inmortalis" with my own bloody finger. I started to make my way down the endless staircase but with each step I began hearing a slushing or splashing sound, after a while I glanced at my feet and noticed that there was a stream of blood going down the stairs which began at the building and continued well ahead of where I was standing. I contemplated turning around and heading back but decided to go forward, but as I took the step I felt a hand on my shoulder which immediately woke me up.

TUESDAY OCTOBER 20ᵀᴴ, 2015

"Juan, are you going to work today?" Brooke whispered into my ear. "It's 10 a.m., did your alarm not go off?"

"Good morning princess, I guess I didn't hear it," I answered. "Thank you for waking me, I'd still be asleep if you didn't wake me up."

"I made Christian some oatmeal," said Brooke, "Do you want some?"

"Sure, thank you," I answered as I turned on the TV.

'We'll have mostly cloudy skies with temperatures in the high 70s for most of the day, perfect for any outdoor activities after work...'

"Brooke, do you have any plans today after dance?" I asked as I took my first bite of oatmeal.

"No, not really why?" she sounded eager to do as much as possible before she was too uncomfortable to do anything.

"I think we should go to the beach," I suggested, "I'm going to an open house with Don Pacho at 2 p.m. but I don't think that will take long, I should be home around 3:30 or 4:00."

"Yes, let's do that!" she answered. "Christian, do you want to go to the beach?" she asked as Christian came bouncing down the stairs.

'In other stories, the investigation on the high rise fire last night in the Kendall area that claimed the lives of five people has stalled due to authorities not linking a name or ownership to the condominium. The condominium's management office declined to comment, more on this developing story later tonight during our 9 p.m. newscast.'

"Well that's strange," commented Brooke.

Damn, there goes the chance of this being a huge coincidence out the window. Decline to comment, sounds like someone is hiding something.

"Sweetie, are you ok?" asked Brooke. "Is something wrong?"

"What, no, why do you ask?" I replied.

"I've had this feeling since last night that something is wrong. You look worried," Brooke added.

"Everything is good, just had a crappy night last night," I answered.

I finished the rest of my breakfast which had gone cold and headed upstairs to get ready.

I can't fool Brooke, she knows me too well. I AM worried, worried that I don't fully know what to do or know how to handle my options without messing something up or creating a dangerous situation for my family. Our lives have changed drastically since we moved to Florida, especially since I began working for Don Pacho. I've grown to look up to him as a mentor. He has given me the opportunity to succeed and create a life where I can fulfill my personal goals, provide for my own family and even help our extended families.

Everything I do is for my family and our future.

On the other hand, does my respect and admiration for my mentor outweigh the possibility that I could be working for someone that just killed FBI or DEA agents? The fact that the DEA could be involved in this could be a sign that Don Pacho is a drug trafficker or at least involved in that world.

But would a businessman that has so much exposure with public businesses and investments risk it all like this? Or is it the perfect cover?

If he is involved in this and he is a drug trafficker, do I contact the police or do I just look the other way? A man like that wouldn't include me in his personal circle if he didn't know everything about me and even kept tabs on me. That would explain how he knew where we lived despite not ever telling him the exact address.

I made it to the office right before lunch time, which gave me the opportunity to sit in an interview with HR and a candidate to fill my previous position. With my promotion I would now have several people reporting to me. We are planning to hire a PR & Marketing person for each one of Don Pacho's businesses that were in the first binder.

"So based on your resume you've done PR & Marketing for a couple of companies for some years?" I asked the interviewee.

"Yes, for the last four years I've been in charge of public relations and marketing for a fitness & nutrition start-up here in Miami," she answered. "But also, I have done the same for my own personal brand since I'm sponsored by the same company."

Don Pacho had asked me to oversee the hiring of all these positions with one special request. He required that all the positions be filled with attractive women or muñecas (dolls) as he called them, between 20 to 30 years old. It definitely made the hiring process harder since I like to focus on finding the right candidates with the right experience, while trying to fulfill his request.

This girl fit both requirements.

I was about to make a job offer when the door suddenly opened and in came Don Pacho.

"Sorry for bursting in and not knocking," he said. "I'm a little early Juancho. Who is this?" he asked, referring to our new employee.

"Chelsea, I would like to introduce you to Don...." Don Pacho interrupted. "Miss, you can call me Don Pacho. I'm the owner of this operation," he grinned from ear to ear.

"Juancho, did she get the job?" he asked while clasping her hand.

"I was just about to offer the position if she's interested in starting right away." I answered.

"So Chelsea, will you be joining us?" he asked her. "I hope you are."

I think the man found his next prey.

"Absolutely, I would be honored to work for you!" she didn't hesitate in accepting the offer.

We welcomed her and excused ourselves out of the room. Before heading out we passed by our accounting department to confirm the check amounts for the Dade County School District and sign them.

I quickly briefed Don Pacho on the donation that we were making to them and asked him to sign the checks.

"Juancho, you're a VP, you sign them!" he ordered. "Alright, let's go."

Don Pacho and I headed to the open house in his pearl white $800,000 Brabus 6X6 with crimson red interior, a more than appropriate ride for this event.

On the way there Don Pacho said that he wanted to discuss with me the idea of either building or buying a new office where we could consolidate all of our employees under one roof. It would definitely make reporting an easier task with my new position. He also mentioned that he wanted me to work with the VP of Operations and be involved in the search and purchase of the new place.

With the current events back at home I couldn't help myself from analyzing each move and word coming out of Don Pacho. Could this guy really be a cold blooded killer?

I must have been staring at him in an unusual way without realizing it.

"Juancho, are you alright?" he asked.

"Yes sir why?" I asked while clearing my throat.

"You have a look on your face that I've never seen on you before," Don Pacho said, "I've only seen that look on cops and detectives."

"I'm sorry Don Pacho, I was just thinking about a possible location for the new office," I quickly tried to change the subject.

"I think downtown Miami would be the ideal place, like the Wells Fargo tower," I spat out the first thing that came to mind.

"Which one is that one?" he asked as he was backing up this behemoth between a Rolls Royce and a McLaren.

"It's the emerald green building overseeing Biscayne Bay. You can see part of it from your backyard," I replied.

Once inside the building Don Pacho introduced me to his contact at Brabus USA. She had been the point of contact when Don Pacho ordered his custom-made monster truck parked outside.

"Don Pacho, how is that 6X6 treating you?" she asked.

"I love it, but do you think I need to fork out another $100K to get some proper cup holders?" he asked sarcastically.

Our main reason for being here today was that Don Pacho was going to be placing an order for a new private jet and wanted the Brabus Aviation division to build it.

I'm not quite sure why he brought me along. I didn't bring anything to the conversation anyway. I excused myself and went to the restroom.

I wondered off into the crowd to check out some of the vehicles on display. Most of these supercars are well above the $200K price tag and just way too expensive. I immediately started smiling after the realization that these cars were technically in my price range now. I am a new millionaire and I do like what Brabus does to already powerful cars in the AMG line.

I had been saving some money to buy a new car since I think it's time to retire my Toyota Corolla. Brooke already has her nice Mercedes SUV compliments of Don Pacho, so I would like to upgrade as well.

"Juancho, why don't you just pick one already?" Don Pacho chuckled as he walked over to me.

"Did you already order your new jet Don Pacho?" I asked.

"I just needed a few questions answered first. The actual order is placed in Germany," he answered. "In fact, I'll need you to clear your schedule this coming weekend. We fly out on Thursday. We'll spend Friday in Germany and make a quick stop in Barcelona on the way back for a meeting." He added.

"Germany and Spain it is sir," I replied.

"We would like to thank all of you for attending our open house today. We are very excited to be in this community and bring a higher standard of supercar from our factories in Germany to the streets of Miami. We invite you to look for our monthly newsletter for upcoming events," said a voice over the building's speaker system, *"We would also like to acknowledge our first sale here tonight from a Mr. Don Pacho who purchased one of our Brabus G700 Widestars. This $300,000 SUV is at the pinnacle of German engineering packed with 700 horsepower and the finest materials for an all-terrain masterpiece, thank you again and until next time."*

"Party is over," Don Pacho said. "Juancho, I've got one more thing to do with you today. I'll need you to drive the new Brabus and follow me to one of my properties in Coral Gables. Can you keep that powerful machine under control?"

Crap, it's already 3:35pm and it will start getting dark at 5, I'll have to cancel the family beach date with Brooke, and Christian David.

"Sure boss." I answered.

A staff member brought the new Brabus out front and handed me the keys. Interesting side note, if I had bought a car tonight, I would've gone for the same one. I have a thing for blacked out cars like this beast. I pressed the self-starter and heard the earth rumble as this thing came alive and several acres of rainforest in the Amazon were flattened instantaneously.

"Juancho, in case we get separated, put this address in your navigation '7275 Old Cutler road, Coral Gables, FL 33143', it's down the street from

Cartagena park," he explained while I entered the information into the screen.

At least we're not too far away. It's only five miles from here.

"*Estimated drive time 17 minutes, turn Left in 0.1 miles*," the Siri-like voice said with a slight German accent.

As we pulled into the main courtyard, past the gates of the house, I noticed that this was - at least from what I could see - a more toned down property from the other mansions I've visited. By no means was it just a house, it was still a mansion, just not as much grandeur as the other ones.

The setting with this house and the two SUVs was straight out of an episode of NARCOS at Hacienda Napoles. If all of what's happening ends up being true then I bet I'm already an accomplice. I'm already being spied on by the feds I might as well indulge a little right?

"What do you think of this one, do you like it?" Don Pacho asked as he walked over to the entrance holding one of the leather binders that I picked up in Park City.

"I love the façade; this is the kind of house that I picture for us one day." I answered as I glanced at my phone with an incoming message from Brooke that simply said 'You suck'.

"That's great Juancho; you always need to aspire for bigger and better things. One of my favorite authors is Langston Hughes and one of his quotes that I live by is this one, '*I have discovered in life that there are ways of getting anywhere you want to go, IF you really want to go*'," Don Pacho read from a page in his little black pocket book.

Don Pacho proceeded to give me a thorough tour of the whole property. A little less than 10 thousand square feet filled with 7 bedrooms, 8 bathrooms, outdoor pool with hot tub, basketball court, wine cellar and even a wishing water fountain in the main courtyard. All of this for a mere $6 million, I hope he's not expecting me to buy this off of him.

"Juancho, let's sit and chat a little. I want to discuss a section of this second binder with you," he said as he signaled me towards the little bistro set near the pool. "Actually, let me get some drinks, what would you like to drink?"

"I'm fine with water, thank you," I answered.

As Don Pacho went inside I glanced at the opened binder and I saw that every page of this section were old discolored maps. They were covered in notes along with longitude and latitude numbers.

"I couldn't find any water bottles, except this Manzana Postobon," he chuckled as he pulled his chair next to mine.

"No worries, I grew up loving Manzana Postobon, thank you," I replied.

"Juancho, do you recall me asking you about having a US or Colombian passport?" he asked.

"Yes, I have an American passport." I said expectantly.

"Juancho, what I'm about to share with you has the potential of making you a very wealthy man. If you play your cards right it will also give you something that is more valuable than money and that is power," Don Pacho said with an emphasis on the word POWER. "The reason why I have you here and no one else is because I trust you. Also I know that you don't take loyalty lightly. I have waited many years for someone I can fully trust and I believe I have that person in you."

As I listened to each individual word that came out of his mouth I could feel my heart race like never before. Is this what anxiety feels like or is this some sort of adrenaline? The words wealth, power, and loyalty kept replaying in my head and seemed to get louder with each second that went by. I have to try to remain quiet, attentive and neutral to everything he is about to show to me.

"Juancho, by accepting the offer that I will be making you in the next few minutes, you will become my right hand man. With this responsibility certain assignments will have to be fulfilled. Your position as a Vice President at this very moment is very limited; therefore this opportunity surpasses the scope of your current job description and is to operate as a

separate venture," he explained.

I could feel sweat beginning to drip down my back as I contemplated on

the magnitude of whatever was coming my way. He wasn't making it easy

for me as he built up the anticipation with his masterful sales pitch.

"We will begin with 60 individual assignments given one at a time. These

assignments are trips to different parts of the world where you will fly to

and manage excavation teams who will retrieve buried barrels. The

barrels will then be placed in cargo planes and flown to Miami and other

locations," he said as he copied some information out of one of the pages

in the binder.

Latitude 6.208053 Longitude -75.718122

GPS Coordinates

6° 12' 28.9908" N75° 43' 5.2392" W

He handed me the paper and it appeared to be coordinates for the first assignment. I took a sip of my drink and continued to look at the coordinates for what felt like an eternity.

"Juancho, do you have any questions?" he asked.

Questions, yeah I have questions. Did you kill and burn FBI or DEA agents? What is the meaning behind this special treatment that you have been giving me for the past year? Are you a drug lord? Am I in danger if I decline? Am I in danger if I accept?

"I have two questions," I replied, "Where will these coordinates take me?"

"El Morrillo, it's a small country town an hour away west of Medellin," he answered, "What's your second question?"

"What's in the barrels?" I asked while analyzing his every move.

After a long pause he smiled and said; "Power."

Does he expect me to fly all over the world and not know exactly what I'm digging up for him?

"$600 million in cash," he added before taking a sip of his beer.

My racing heart stopped. "You have $600 million buried in the ground!?" I exclaimed.

"At each site," he clarified.

My heart started racing again. I pulled out my cell phone and opened the calculator.

"That's $36 billion," I murmured to myself in disbelief.

"Juancho, at the end of the 60 assignments you will receive one percent of the total amount as payment," he said.

It was simple math but I had to see it with my own eyes. One percent equals $360 million. I would be PAID $360 million?!

"I don't want you to rush into this without thinking it over and possibly discussing it with your wife," he chuckled, "I do however want to give you a couple of incentives as motivation."

He picked up the keys for the new Brabus off the table and placed them in my hands along with the keys for the house.

"Juancho, I have to go, but you can stay, it's your house anyway. I'll give you 24 hours to make a decision," he said as he finished his beer, picked up his things and excused himself.

I remained seated staring into the pool water for what must have been an hour, but I soon realized that the pool lights had been on for a while. I looked at my watch and it had been almost three hours since Don Pacho left.

I stepped inside my new fully furnished mansion still not knowing what to think. What in the world am I going to do? I walked through the whole house again hoping to instantaneously know what to do, how to explain things to Brooke, how to explain things to myself for that matter. There is no way that all this comes from clean money. $600 million buried in each site, are you freaking kidding me?

I looked at my phone to read an incoming text from Brooke.

'Juan, are you cheating on me? Where are you, it's almost 9 p.m.!' asked Brooke, *'I need your help with Christian.'*

I quickly apologized and texted that no, I was not cheating on her, but to answer her question, I would simply have to show her. *'I'm on my way home princess. I'll be there in 15 min.'*

As I closed the main entrance door and walked over to my new $300K SUV, I noticed something on the hood. Don Pacho had left the gate/garage opener on top of a piece of paper. I read the note as I got in and it said *'Garbage day is Friday, remember to recycle Juancho'*, a little humor from the boss.

When I made it home I was greeted by Batman. Christian David loved his new Halloween costume and would sleep in it if it was up to him. "Sorry Brooke, it took way longer than I expected," I explained.

"What were you doing?" she asked, "Didn't you say it was just an open house?"

"Yeah, but Don Pacho had a change of plans after the open house," I said.

"So his changes of plans dictate our lives entirely now?" she complained.

"Princess, I'm sorry. Let me make it up to you. How's dinner tomorrow night?" I asked as I put my arms around her and rested my hands on her cute baby bump.

"Okay, but can it be just you and me?" she asked, "My sister is ok watching Christian tomorrow night."

"Definitely princess," I answered.

"Great. It's funny how every time that I make a nice dinner you either come home late or you're not hungry," she added, "I made some arepas for you."

"I love the arepas that you make," I said as I walked over to the kitchen.

"Before you sit down to eat, I need you to brush Christian's teeth, read with him and put him to bed please," the Madame ordered.

After the nightly routine of putting this kid down for the night I took a few minutes to slow my mind down and really think at what my options were. Was I really prepared to do what was necessary for Don Pacho? Better yet, was I prepared to turn down such an offer? I had truly hit the jackpot with Don Pacho, but there were so many factors to consider. Could I be dealing with possible jail time or worse yet, possibly death?

Well, so much for slowing my mind down.

I pulled out my phone and my earbuds to avoid waking Christian David up. Since I had fallen asleep last time while watching NARCOS, I decided to restart the episode again so I wouldn't miss a minute. I was halfway through the episode when a scene involving Pablo Escobar made me drop my phone on my face. I suddenly couldn't breathe, my mind and heart collectively started racing out of control. I stared at the screen, had to rewind and replay the scene over and over. I couldn't believe what I was seeing.

Pablo Escobar had his men dig holes throughout Colombia to hide billions of dollars using plastic barrels. He had a guy in the Medellin Cartel named Black Beard keep notes with latitude and longitude coordinates for the location of each site.

Could my personal belief and that of millions of Colombians, about Pablo Escobar's death be true? Could Don Pacho really be the living Escobar? I've always said that the guy's death was simple, too simple for someone with so much power. He could have easily faked his death, escaped and be living like a king in South Beach or the South of France.

Don Pacho definitely fits the bill; he has the lifestyle of royalty and likes to flaunt it as often as possible. But could this just be a huge coincidence? Maybe he does have some sort of infatuation with Escobar, the Medellin cartel and simply wanted to emulate them. But what am I talking about? We're dealing with billions of dollars buried all over the world, buried for at least a couple of decades. Very few people in this world have access to this type of wealth and especially have a need to hide it from everyone.

I stepped out of Christian David's bedroom and headed downstairs in search of a notepad.

I started going through all of the many interactions that I've had with Don Pacho since day one, and I quickly started to find shocking similarities with Escobar. All things led to the most powerful drug lord that this world has seen and supposedly been nonexistent since 1993. He is alive, is now my current employer and he just offered me the role of his right hand man.

Maybe those dead DEA agents were checking me out as a way to get to him and simply got too close to uncovering this monstrous truth before they got wiped out.

I quickly glanced at my watch and noticed that it was 4:58 a.m. I had been at this the whole night to the point of not wanting to sleep. I pulled out my laptop and read several dozen publications and sites about Escobar. I think I clicked on every link and video that came up about him.

There was no doubt that no one knew what I knew. I can only imagine the magnitude of this information. This would definitely be one of the biggest news stories of 2015 or of the last 20 years for that matter but I can't tell a soul, not even Brooke.

The way I see it, I think I only have two options. I picked up the pen and tried to narrow down my thoughts as much as I could before making what could be one of the biggest decisions in my life.

On one hand I would have the financial future secured of not only my wife and kids, but the economic stability for every generation to come after I'm gone. However, that could easily come with some consequences I don't know of yet. What's the worst that could happen? Well, I could end up like those DEA agents for one. If I don't end up dead then I may end up in jail for who knows how long. Am I willing to go all in? Is doing it for the family good enough for a justification?

Now option two, Don Pacho is already paying me $5 million a year as his new Vice President. That's $5 million for fulfilling my job description which most likely does not bring any life threatening requirements or have the potential of sending me to prison. Is an additional $360 million really worth the risk?

What about the "power" that Don Pacho mentioned? I'm beginning to doubt that he's referring to the buying power that money has. If he really is who I think he is, then that power is what terrorized an entire country for several decades with bombings, kidnappings, murders, and was an integral part of the most powerful criminal organization this planet has ever seen in its history.

Now that I think about it, the internet said that the guy had a net worth of $30 billion when he died, but that's without counting the $36 billion that he's having me dig up. Plus it's been 22 years since those numbers were made public. He must have just as much or more than Bill Gates and Carlos Slim, that's 80 billion dollars plus. I guess the exact amount would depend if whether he continued trafficking or not in these last two decades.

"Juan, why are you up so early?" asked a yawning Brooke as she entered the kitchen.

"I couldn't sleep," I answered.

"You never went to bed?" she asked surprised. "What are you doing on your computer?"

"Some stuff for work," I replied. "Actually, I want to talk to you about some of this tonight during our date."

"Alright, where are we eating?" she asked.

"It's the db Bistro Moderne on the ground level of the Wells Fargo building downtown," I said while turning off the laptop and folding the list I had been compiling for hours. "Why are you up so early?"

"I wanted to get a work out in before heading to the studio this morning."

She answered. "We have an early morning meeting. It seems that the

owners of the studio are thinking about selling the studio, and even

offered all the Directors an opportunity to buy it before taking offers from

external bidders."

"If I had the money I would totally do it. We would already have three

locations with a solid membership base." Brooke added. "If only we had a

couple of million stashed away, right?"

Man, if only she knew the kind of money heading our way if I go through

with this offer. I can see now how Don Pacho has so many businesses

aside from his many investments. He must be doing some serious money

laundering. Would I have to do the same?

I guess I could just start all the different business ideas I've had in the past

but couldn't due to the lack of capital. Owning a dance studio is on the list

of businesses I would want to have in our portfolio and Brooke could

manage it. Look at me, now I'm contemplating money laundering. This is

madness, the only illegal thing I ever did was steal a pack of gum when I was 5-years-old and I felt like crap afterwards. That's quite the jump from a pack of gum to money laundering.

"Princess, I need to sleep, I'm going to bed for a bit," I said. "Can you please wake me up in a couple of hours?"

"Are you not going in today?" Brooke asked.

"Yeah, but I need a short nap at least," I answered.

It didn't feel like I had been asleep for even an hour when Brooke woke me up.

"Juan, it's 2 p.m.," she whispered.

"Why didn't you wake me up earlier, I said only a couple of hours princess," I exclaimed.

"You looked like you needed a little longer than a couple of hours," she replied. "Are you still going in to work?"

"Nah, at this point there's no need. Our dinner reservation is at 4 p.m." I added.

"Why so early?" Brooke asked.

"I want to take you to a place after dinner and I'm hoping that we still have some light," I said referring to my plans of taking her to our mansion. I can't keep all of this from Brooke, if I did I don't think I'd be able to keep it to myself for long. I'm pretty sure that she'll be against it but she needs to know.

Once we were ready and on our way down to get the car, I realized that in a couple of minutes I would have the opportunity to see a brief preview of how the night was going to go. I was going to witness Brooke's reaction to the new SUV, surprise number 1 out of 5 for the night. At dinner I was going to tell her how I had received another pay raise this time to $5 million a year, how we now were the proud owners of a Coral Gables mansion, how Don Pacho had extended a $360 million gig to me, and oh yes, how I came to believe that Don Pacho is actually the most powerful and richest drug lord in the history of humanity who came back from the dead.

As we walked over to the new ride I pressed the automatic starter and waited to see her response, but nothing. I opened the door for her but she still didn't seem surprised, in fact I was more surprised for her lack of surprise. She simply got in without a word and buckled in.

As we pulled out of our building I kept thinking that maybe this was a way to show her disapproval, but wait disapproval of what?

"Alright, are you not curious? You're not going to say anything?" I asked in amazement.

"Actually I was wondering why it took so long for you to get a car from him, aren't you his favorite?" she said. "I was beginning to think that he liked me better than you."

I guess she has a point. Her reaction leads me to believe that just maybe she'll react similarly to the other surprises, because the simple truth is that I want everything but I feel stuck or somewhat unsure, call it a moral dilemma. All comes down to the notion of accepting drug money, but not all of it should be categorized as drug money, he has started multiple companies that are very successful. However, that can only be said about the source of my new $5 million salary and not the $360 million.

As we pulled up to the valet Brooke asked me the price of the car and then made a comment about how our neighbors were going to begin growing suspicious on what we really did for a living.

"I guess we'll just have to move to a richer area then, don't you agree?" I said as I took her hand and helped her out.

"Honey, I think you have to make a little bit more money before we consider moving again," she replied.

"Yeah, I guess we do," I chuckled.

"Would you like to sit inside or outside?" asked our hostess. "We have heaters outside."

"Are you okay with outside princess?" I asked.

"Sure, as long as it's not too cold." She replied.

After settling in and looking over the menu for a good amount of time, we decided to start with some Alsatian Tarte Flambée and the Soupe du Jour followed by some appetizing entrees. I contemplated telling her the first topic for discussion of the night but I decided to wait until it was time for dessert. Instead I mentioned how Don Pacho had assigned me to look for a new location for an office and that I was going to look into this building.

As we were being served our entrees I happened to glance at the reflection on a nearby window and I thought I saw Don Pacho's white 6X6 going around the corner but by the time I turned around it was gone.

"What is it?" Brooke asked due to my sudden reaction.

"Nothing, I thought I saw a car I like," I responded.

I still have a couple of hours to make my decision, I doubt Don Pacho would be that anxious for my answer and see the need to come all the way here to make sure that I'm not getting cold feet. He has waited decades for this moment so he'll have to wait until I call him tonight.

"A car you like?" she asked surprised. "You want something more expensive than that tank that you're driving now?"

"You're right princess, it is a tank but I'll be content with it for some time," I answered. "I gave it a name by the way, the Tumbler."

"The Tumbler, isn't Batman supposed to be quiet like a ninja?" Brooke asked referring to the loudness of my new ride. "You can hear that thing from a mile away."

While we enjoyed our dinner we talked about a few subjects that we still hadn't had time to focus on. First her job as a Director at the studio and her schedule for some upcoming productions, Christian David's introduction to preschool in January, the pregnancy and the to-do list that comes along with the arrival of a new member of the family, and finally our Thanksgiving plans for flying back to Utah to spend time with both families.

"Will you be enjoying one of our desserts tonight?" our waiter asked as he handed us a menu.

"Of course they will!" said a voice coming from behind our waiter. "You can't celebrate without dessert."

It was Don Pacho accompanied by a couple of girls no more than half his age.

"Brooke, always a pleasure seeing you," Don Pacho said.

"Don Pacho what a surprise," I said as I took a drink of water. "What brings you around here?"

"Just wanted to take these lovely ladies out before I started getting ready for our trip tomorrow," he answered.

"I hope you're packed." He added referring to me.

"Excuse me, what trip?" Brooke asked surprised. "Where are you going?"

"I can see that your husband hasn't told you yet," said Don Pacho, "I'll let your husband tell you, we'll be on our way, enjoy the rest of the night," he added as he kissed Brooke on the cheek.

"Juancho, I'll expect your call in a bit?" he winked.

As Don Pacho and his female entourage walked away from our table, I was left with Brooke giving me a raised eye brow.

"Hey princess, don't look at me like that; I was planning on telling you while we ate dessert," I explained.

I went ahead and ordered the Bourbon S'more, the Chocolate Fondant and the Crunchy Chocolate Bar with Dulce de Leche ice cream. I guess in a way I was getting ready to touch on some delicate topics so I needed plenty of desserts to sweeten the conversation.

"Three desserts, I don't think you'll get off this easy Juan," warned Brooke, "Tell me about this trip and what we're celebrating."

I explained to Brooke how Don Pacho and I would be going on a quick trip to Germany to place an order for his new custom jet. We would also make a quick stop in Barcelona before heading back to the States. I agreed with her that I really didn't have a reason to be going and leaving my pregnant wife behind, but I explained that Don Pacho needed me to come along for some unknown reason.

"Here are your desserts, enjoy!" our waiter said. "Anything else I can get you both?"

"We're good, thanks," Brooke replied.

"Ok, now you can tell me what we're celebrating Juan," she asked with an inquisitive tone.

"Do you have a pen in your purse?" I asked.

"A pen for what?" she asked.

"So I can show you," I replied.

Since I didn't know how to start the conversation I decided to show her visually. I took a napkin, wrote $5,000,000 on it and slid it across the table.

"What's this?" she asked while glancing at my note.

"It's my new yearly salary princess," I chuckled.

"What do you mean your new salary?" she asked again, obviously stunned.

"You heard me right Brooke, Don Pacho gave me a raise from $120 thousand a year to $5 million starting this pay period," I explained. "You're looking at the new VP of Marketing & Public Relations for all of Don Pacho's business ventures."

Brooke continued to eat her dessert silently while I explained how Don Pacho had shown up unannounced a couple of days ago to our home and had extended the promotion to me. I shared how the salary negotiation went down with him, and finally I touched on some of the duties that came with the new role.

She continued to stare at her dessert without a word.

"Well, what do you think?" I asked trying to get a sense of what she was thinking.

"To tell you the truth I'm not quite sure how to feel. I'm excited for your promotion but I don't know about the money?" Brooke replied. "Can this really be happening to us?"

"Princess, it was really hard for me to grasp what was going on as well you know," I explained. "We've had a series of unreal events one after another, and when we think that it can't get better than this Don Pacho proves us wrong."

"I agree that it sounds crazy Brooke, but things like this can really happen and it's happening to us," I added.

"Well sweetie, I trust you," said Brooke as she held my hand, "If you say this is all real and your boss is not setting some unusual expectations from you then I support you 100%."

To only think that our evening still contained a few more surprises of this caliber, my heart began to race quite a bit.

We finished enjoying the rest of our desserts while I asked our waiter for the check. To our surprise the waiter informed us that Don Pacho had already covered our dinner for the night and had asked the staff to give Brooke a bouquet of flowers on our way out. It was obvious that Don Pacho was buttering us up before making our decision.

"So becoming millionaires is what we were really celebrating tonight right?" asked Brooke as we waited for the valet to pull the Tumbler around.

"Believe it or not, it's actually not the only thing that we're celebrating tonight," I said. "There are still a few more things I need to show you."

We made the quick drive on Dixie Hwy heading to Coral Gables and even passed Brooke's dance studio on our way to the house. I think I surprised her with a side comment I made on how we should really consider buying the studio now. I could sense her excitement build up at the simple idea of becoming the owner of her own studio. She quickly did the numbers and mentioned how we could pay it off in less than a year with the $400K plus a month that would begin coming in soon.

Brooke's plan sounded like a good plan by all means, but an even better and more efficient plan would be to pay it off in one lump sum. No monthly payments or anything like that, just a cash transaction and it's ours. One simple trip to pick up the boss' money would pay me $6 million in cash.

As we pulled in past the gate and parked in front of the house Brooke made a comment on how she was hoping that I wasn't thinking about buying this house. She loved telling me how my eyes are bigger than my stomach and that I always go for the most expensive stuff. What can I say, I do have expensive taste and working for Don Pacho certainly hasn't helped.

I spent a few minutes playing realtor and gave her a detailed walk through of the house and grounds.

"Do you want to get in the hot tub princess?" I asked.

"Sure, but you still haven't told me why you have the keys to this house Juan?" an inquisitive Brooke asked.

"Don't worry Brooke I'm not buying the house if that's what you want to hear," I replied. "Let's get the skinny dipping started and we can keep talking."

"What do you think of the house?" I asked while helping her into the water. "Would you want a house like this someday?"

"Of course, who wouldn't?" she replied, "The house is beautiful!"

"Is it one of Don Pacho's houses?" she asked.

"It is until tonight," I answered. "More like for the next hour or so."

"What do you mean for the next hour or so?" she asked.

"Princess, Don Pacho is giving us this house based on what we decide to do in the next hour," I explained. "Actually this house and the Tumbler are part of the same package. They're for us to keep as incentives."

"Incentives for what?" she asked the million dollar question.

I went and explained every detail of what the gig consisted of without leaving any detail out. I was about to go into the whole thing of how I believed that Don Pacho was the resurrected Pablo Escobar but I decided to leave that part for another time. It was already a lot of information to take in and we had to make a decision within the next couple of hours.

After a lengthy pause she broke the silence.

"Did you already say yes to him?" she asked.

"I haven't, I'm supposed to call him in the next hour or so with our decision." I said.

"I don't think you should do it," she said. "There's obviously a reason why that money has been hidden like that for such a long time."

"It also makes perfect sense why he has been treating us so well for this whole time," she added. "He's been polishing you and building your loyalty towards him so that you can't say no."

"What are you going to do?" asked Brooke.

"Well, that's why we're here, I wanted to tell you all this so that we can both make a decision," I replied.

"Juan, the truth is that no matter what I say, if this is something you want to do you'll get your way," she said. "I don't think you should do it. The safety of our family or you going to jail is not worth $360 million; however it's your choice since you're the patriarch of this family."

The moment of truth finally came so I excused myself, wrapped a towel around my waist and went inside the house to make the call.

"Good evening Don Pacho, I'm in," I confirmed. "What time should I meet you at the airport tomorrow morning?"

"Your decision makes me very happy Juancho," he replied. "Don't worry about driving to the airport; I'll have one my guys pick you up at 9:30 a.m."

Alright Juan, there is no turning back now from this point forward. You better be ready.

"So what did you tell him?" Brooke asked while I joined her in the hot tub again.

"I'm doing it!" I answered. "I'll do the 60 trips, collect my payment and once I've completed the assignment, that's it."

"So Mrs. Arias, you are now the owner of a 6 million dollar Coral Gables mansion," I whispered in her ear and pulled her close to me. "I say we continue the celebrating right here."

THURSDAY OCTOBER 22ND, 2015

I woke up this morning full of energy despite the long night we had celebrating. I had time for a quick run and put a suitcase together for the trip. According to Don Pacho we would return to Miami on Sunday or Monday I believe.

While eating breakfast I received a text message from the boss asking me to bring my Bayern Munich jersey. Apparently one of his business contacts had a private suite for the Borussia Dortmund v. Bayern Munich match this Saturday afternoon. We'll be visiting the Brabus headquarters in Bottrop which according to Google Maps is only a 40 minute drive from

where we'll be staying in Dortmund. I guess that's another item on my
bucket list that I can cross off.

At exactly 9:30 a.m. I received a phone call from my driver letting me
know that he was downstairs. I hugged and kissed my favorite people and
headed downstairs.

When we made it to the north end of the Miami International airport, I'm
not going to lie, I loved the sense of power that Don Pacho had
mentioned. Here I am coming out of a chauffeured Rolls Royce Phantom
in a business suit about to get in a private jet en route to Europe, and not
only that, by the end of 2016 I will have a personal net worth of more
than $360 million. To think that a year ago I was a full-time supervisor at
the carwash making less than $40K a year is sort of a rags to riches story
in a way.

Since Don Pacho wasn't here yet, I was welcomed in by Don Pacho's pilot
who asked to take my luggage.

"Mr. Arias, can I offer you anything to drink?" the stewardess asked.

"I'll have some orange juice and a bottle of water please," I answered as I heard a loud rev from Don Pacho's Bugatti Veyron.

I glanced out the window and noticed that he wasn't alone. Following him was one of his other drivers in the other Rolls Royce with four female passengers. Man, this guy can't keep it in his pants for very long, now he has to bring these chicks along with us. If only Brooke knew who I'm traveling with for the next 11 hours in a small enclosure.

"Good morning Juancho, a little overdressed aren't we?" asked Don Pacho. "I doubt you want to be in a suit for the next 11 hours."

"Anyway, I want to introduce these fine looking ladies to you," Don Pacho said as he had each girl introduce herself to me. "Two for me and two for you!"

"Don Pacho, thank you for thinking of me but I don't think Brooke would like that," I chuckled.

"Well, she's not here so let me know if you change your mind," he added as the crew began closing the jet's door.

I had a feeling that this was going to be a long flight, not only due to the distance but mainly because of whom I was sealed up with. Don Pacho is quite the womanizer and it's no secret that he enjoys throwing frequent orgies at his pad. Then again, I'm no expert on orgies but I believe that an orgy consists of several men and women. His parties consist of just him and multiple women at the same time. I'm not surprised if he pulls something like that here or at some point on the trip.

Once we were at cruising speed Don Pacho sat directly across from me with a glass of wine. He began telling me how these four girls were all fitness models and had huge followings on social media primarily on Instagram. He's like a senior frat boy preying on the freshmen girls. I'm surprised he hasn't been diagnosed with some type of STD yet. It wouldn't be a complete shock to me if he spends more time sleeping around with women that he does sleeping or eating.

"Juancho, let's change subjects a little shall we?" he said. "Have you given any thought to when you would complete the first pick up?"

"I was thinking about the first week of November," I answered. "Is that ok with you Don Pacho?"

"That works for me," he replied. "When we get back I'll get in contact with the team that you'll be managing and letting them know of your arrival."

"So after we dig up the money, what happens next?" I asked as one of the girls wearing just lingerie sat on Don Pacho's lap.

"Be a sweetheart and give me a foot massage would you?" he asked the girl who disappeared as she slid under the table.

"Juancho, the money will be placed in a cargo plane at a nearby airport and transported to a different location," he answered. "If you're wondering about your $6 million payment for each job, it will be ready for you once you return home from each trip."

"I guess my next question has already been answered, but are we just supposed to go in and out that easy?" I asked.

"We have the right people in the right institutions paid off so it shouldn't…." he paused in mid-sentence and closed his eyes.

After about half a minute of just dead silence I noticed that the girl under the table wasn't only giving him a foot massage. We haven't even been in the air 30 minutes and they've already turned the plane into a brothel.

"You shouldn't run into any problems or delays," he resumed as he cleared his throat and the girl reappeared. "If a situation arose in one of your trips, the men that you're managing are trained and equipped to deal with it."

OK, so pretty much what he's saying is that the men I'll be managing are trained killers and if any obstacle arises they will just blow them away. That's a new bit of information that had not come up in previous conversations.

"Hey Juan, would you like me to give you a foot massage?" asked one of the other half-naked girls as she squeezed in my chair.

Don Pacho just stared at me with a smirk.

"Thank you but I'll pass; I'm not a fan of foot massages," I replied to her offer.

"You don't know what you're missing out on my friend," Don Pacho chuckled.

We continued our chat for a couple of more hours. He went into detail on the first 10 assignments including locations and dates. The first five pick-ups were all within Colombia. My first one in November would be near Medellin but the other four were spread out throughout the rest of the country. One of the locations was further up north near Sincelejo, the next one was southwest by Pasto, and the last two were by Buenaventura on the pacific coast and the outskirts of Cucuta to the east.

The next five were outside of Colombia starting with the Dominican Republic, followed by Uruguay, Ivory Coast, Portugal and Greece. It's definitely insane how he had this type of money buried around the world to nobody else's knowledge but his and now mine. I asked him how nobody has ever run into any of these sites to what he answered *'It's one of the reasons why I've always invested in real estate."*

After a late lunch I decided to get some actual work done especially since I am a VP after all. I still hadn't sent a few introductory emails to the many people working under me. Before getting to it I realized that I didn't want to spend all 11 hours in a suit so I decided to change. The restroom towards the front of the plane was being used so I headed to the back of the jet which meant that I had to pass the little bedroom area. Just as I expected, Don Pacho and the four chicks were going at it pretty good.

"I knew you would change your mind Juancho!" exclaimed Don Pacho. "There is plenty to go around."

"No thanks boss, don't mind me, I just need to use the restroom," I explained.

I locked myself in the restroom and tried to take as long as possible changing. I dreaded having to come out to a scene straight out of National Geographic. I decided to take out my phone to browse my Facebook feed when the door suddenly swung open. Three of the girls rushed the restroom, jumped on me trying to hold me down to remove my clothes but I was able to set myself free just as one of them started unzipping my pants.

"Ladies, please understand that I'm not interested in joining in, I'm married and I want to keep it that way," I said as I zipped my pants back up. "Don Pacho, can you please leave me out of it?"

I went back to my seat and opened my email. I even had to put headphones on since the moaning and screaming made it impossible to focus.

After another couple of hours working I finally had to get some shut eye, even though I felt the need to sleep with one eye open in case one of these crazies decided to jump me again.

I must have been pretty tired because the next thing I heard was the

pilot's voice announcing that we had started our initial decent. I must

have slept for five hours or so. I glanced over my shoulder and saw two of

the girls sitting directly across from me; they appeared to be pretty

hammered. I'm not carrying these chicks out.

FRIDAY OCTOBER 23RD, 2015 – DORTMUND, GERMANY

Once we landed, four blacked-out Range Rovers were waiting for us. A

few of the men waiting for us went in to get the passed out groupies and

put them together in one of the SUVs. Don Pacho and I were directed to

another SUV where there was a man already sitting inside. He spoke

perfect Spanish but with a slight German accent.

"Amigos, how was your flight?" he asked. "Based on the girls it seems that

you had fun."

"I'm sorry, I haven't introduced myself properly," he smiled and shook my

hand. "My name is Gustavo Ledher but you can call me Gus."

Gus Ledher, Ledher as in Carlos Ledher top member of the Medellin Cartel and first one to be extradited to the US back in the 80s. What would the DEA and Colombian government give to know of this meeting? Gus must be a brother or cousin and this is definitely cocaine money.

All the years growing up in Utah and having to correct people when they assumed that just for being Colombian I would immediately have some sort of connection with the cartels, it now becomes a reality. I am part of this one way or another, at least until I collect my money.

"Gentlemen, you will be staying in the penthouse of my new building in downtown Dortmund," said Gus. "It's a new construction with a five-star hotel, high end restaurants and the best shopping in the downtown area."

The sun was beginning to peek through the morning clouds as we were dropped off at the hotel. We were taken to the 50th floor penthouse overseeing the whole city including Signal Iduna Park where Dortmund will be playing Bayern on Saturday.

"Gentlemen, please put the ladies in those bedrooms," Gus instructed his men.

"Would you like to have breakfast served in the next few minutes?" he asked Don Pacho and me.

"Juancho, I'm going to bed for a bit, it's up to you," Don Pacho said.

"Thank you Gus, but I think I will go downstairs to use the gym." I answered. "I slept pretty well on the way here."

"Great, if you guys need anything don't hesitate to ask your butler or any of the help," Gus explained. There was a crew of five or six people overseeing each of the penthouses.

"Please tell your boss that we will see you tonight at my club to discuss business," added Gus. "I will have my men wait for you downstairs to take you there at 9 p.m."

I made my way down to the gym which was on the 25th and 26th floors. It had a massive infinity pool wrapping around half of the building. As I walked past the pool area making my way to a treadmill I noticed that one of the flat screen TVs had the BBC reporting on an increased rate of car thefts throughout Europe but primarily in Spain and Germany. I started jogging while watching the rest of the report.

"German representatives of the Bundesbank, the German Central Bank, believe that there is a direct connection between the increase in automobile thefts and the increase in trafficking of illicit drugs, human slavery and weapons in European nations."

No obvious coincidence that our stops during this trip happen to be in Spain and Germany. But what I do not understand is the connection between all these, unless they're using stolen cars to transport all of these things making it easier to avoid the authorities between nations.

After my run I decided to get a protein shake at the bar while I did a quick search on Google for 'Drug trafficking in Europe'. I read a couple of articles that repeated some of the statements made on TV. One of the articles mentioned how for example in Germany money transfers had a cap on how much you could transfer. Any amount above €12,499 euros has to be reported to the Bundesbank thus allowing the German authorities to monitor all transactions. It should be interesting to see how Don Pacho will go about buying his new jet.

I made my way up to the penthouse to shower and get my swim trunks. The air felt somewhat cool like a southern California beach, so swimming wasn't out of the question. Now that I think about it I didn't pack any trunks. Once I made it to the penthouse Don Pacho and his female posse were eating breakfast.

"Juancho, the gym on vacation?" he asked. "So you're one of those guys then?"

"Well, help yourself because the girls want to head down to the pool soon." He added.

"Juan, come with us," insisted one of the girls. "We need someone to take care of us if we get any perverts down at the pool."

"Ladies, I want to but I didn't bring any trunks." I replied.

"Juancho, don't worry, I didn't either," said Don Pacho. "Simply take a look at that magazine by the phone, pick a swimsuit your size and call reception."

"They'll bring it up for you." He added.

I glanced at the magazine and the available swimwear was from Dolce & Gabbana. I might be a millionaire now but I'm not spending $250-$400 on swimwear simply for the name.

"Wow, kind of pricey for swim shorts," I chuckled.

"Juancho, you'll be worth a little over a quarter billion dollars soon and you're complaining on the price?" Don Pacho exclaimed. "Don't worry; everything in that magazine is free for us."

Alright, I still can't justify it but I guess I'll get the cheapest ones starting at $250.

"Juan, you should get those!" said two of the girls pointing at the $400 pair. "You'll look really hot with those."

After ordering my new designer shorts that looked more like something that Cristiano Ronaldo would wear, I decided to hit the shower to rinse off the sweat, but before I jumped in I sent a quick Whatsapp message to Brooke.

I made sure that the door was locked just in case the four sexual predators outside decided to break in. I'm not a fan of hot showers or a steamy bathroom, but it seemed appropriate after a five mile run. I was washing off the shampoo when I felt two naked bodies sandwich me. These chicks are insane.

"Ladies, what do I need to do to get the message across to you?" I asked as I continued washing off the shampoo. I surprised myself at how calm I sounded rather than freaking out like I did in the jet. These girls are pure trouble; they are really trying to break me down and a man can only withstand so much.

"Relax Juan; we just wanted to give you your shorts." They replied as one of them slid her finger down my chest. "We thought you might need some help in here."

Once out of the shower we all headed down to the pool. It seemed like all eyes were on us, or at least on the girls. We made camp in one of the hot tubs that must have been made to sit four people but of course, we were six. With a girl on each side I could only imagine Brooke's reaction to all of this madness I found myself in. I barely had finished that thought when almost automatically all four took off their tops.

"Ladies, could you please give us a few minutes?" asked Don Pacho. "We need to discuss a few things."

"Juancho two things, first I want you to understand how glad I am to have you here with me," he said. "And second, I want you to be 100% informed on all the topics that we'll be discussing tonight with Gus and some of his associates."

As I was already suspecting, he opened up about the full operation including the true meaning of our trip to Germany and Spain. He gave me a bogus story of how he got involved into the drug trafficking world without realizing it. According to him in the year 2000, ten years after he initially acquired his transportation business he realized that some of his employees were smuggling drugs from Colombia and Venezuela into Europe by way of Spanish coastal port cities like Malaga, Valencia and Barcelona. Part of the operation also consisted of cargo ships out of Recife, Brazil and into Western Africa. The cargo would then make it up to Morocco and then smuggled into Europe through the strait of Gibraltar.

Tonight's meeting at Gus' club would be with the top 10 heads representing various regions throughout Europe. They all reported to Gus and Gus to Don Pacho. It has been more than 20 years since Pablo was "killed" but the reality is that he continues to be El Capo de Capos and I work for him.

"Do you have any questions about tonight or anything else Juancho?" he asked as he lit up a Cuban cigar.

I do but how to put it in words without giving away that I know who he really is. The last thing I need is for him to know and put my family in real danger.

"I do." I replied. "I still don't understand where the $36 billion come from."

After a long pause, a couple of puffs from his cigar and a stare into my very soul he broke his silence.

"Juancho, everything in due time," He answered as he signaled the girls to come back. "We'll come back to this after you complete the pickups."

"When that day comes, the $360 million will seem like pennies compared to what you'll be earning," he added with a smirk.

As the girls rejoined us in the hot tub all I could think about was how Don Pacho had just offered to make me a billionaire. I began to question whether I would really have it in me to simply walk away after the 60 trips were completed - Would it be insane to decline such an offer or much more insane to accept? Now I'm pretty positive that he's preparing me to play a role in all of this. Could he be thinking of me as his replacement in the long run?

After a couple of hours messing around it finally came time to get ready for tonight's meeting. As instructed by Gus, we had his men drive us to his club where we would be meeting some major players.

Upon arrival we were welcomed in by his staff and led to the VIP section of the club. The VIP room had been reserved entirely for this meeting and each of the ten heads had their posse present. My guess is that the room had a little fewer than 100 people, most of them bodyguards and their women. It was clear that this get-together was not a social event but rather a serious business meeting. There were no introductions or any kind of pleasantries between anyone. Everyone simply took their seat and listened to Gus go through the numbers. The whole thing had a feeling of a sales meeting, the only difference being that the sales personnel here were all armed and the figures being discussed were in the billions.

While listening to one of the reports, I thought to myself that even though the Medellin cartel might have been dismantled back in the 90s, in reality it has morphed into a global cartel and Escobar has been pulling the strings from a backseat position for the last two decades. However, I do wonder if any of these men, aside from Gus, know who Don Pacho really is.

The topics discussed in the 3-hour meeting included all the ones mentioned in the BBC report I had seen earlier today plus some additional ones. One of them focused on the buying off of high executives belonging to institutions like the Bundesbank in Germany and similar institutions throughout the European Union. The next guy gave the growth numbers from the previous year on all imported goods originating from Colombia and referenced them to the 2011 numbers from when the free trade pact with the EU began. The products included flowers, coffee, sugar, fruits, pork, poultry, corn and rice.

It's pretty interesting that these men have built multi-billion dollar companies in all of these various industries and have done it legally. However, the quest for more money has them risking their necks every day. All of these men could make a great living and retirement solely on the importing of these goods. But what am I saying, I'm in this too; I can live like a king with a guaranteed $5 million a year just doing my job, but instead I'm going after the big money and immersing myself in all this.

Once the meeting was over I decided to get some water and started making my way to the bar. As I inched myself across the crowded dance floor, I suddenly felt a hand grab my package and turn me around. It was two of Don Pacho's girls who recognized me despite being wasted.

"Juan, dance with us." One of the girls slurred.

"Maybe later ladies," I answered as I walked away.

After getting groped I finally made it across to the bar and ordered a bottle of water. I glanced at my phone to check if Brooke had answered my Whatsapp message. She did. She mentioned how they had gone on a small family date to the beach and while it was cold, Christian David had a blast. She also said that she had begun looking up ticket prices to fly back to Utah for Thanksgiving. I texted back telling her not to buy anything since Don Pacho was giving us full use of his private jet for the holiday. Lastly she mentioned how the first deposit of $200K had been deposited into our account.

I finished my message by telling them how much I loved them and to not go crazy with the money. I was only kidding, Brooke has always been more careful with money. I'm the one who needs control once in a while.

I had just sent my message when the other two girls joined me. One of them seemed upset but I wasn't able to hear as to why due to the music. The girl closest to me leaned in to explain when I noticed that a couple of guys approached the other girl and one of them groped her from behind. Before she could even turn around I had already jumped out of my seat and had taken the guy down with a single punch. The second man tried to retaliate but I quickly had him in an arm lock against the bar. I suddenly felt a gun to my head from the first guy.

"Let him go hero!" yelled the bloody man in a heavy Russian accent.

I released the guy and slowly backed away.

"Let's see how you deal with gun," he said while he cocked his gun.

As soon as I heard the click something took ahold of me. In one fluid motion I disarmed him, knocked out the guy who I had in an arm lock, and now it was me holding the gun to the Russian's head. By now the music had stopped, the lights had been turned on, and the crowd had dispersed.

"Juancho, what in the world is going on here?" asked Don Pacho who was standing in front of me alongside Gus and a man from the meeting.

Gus explained that the two men I had taken out were bodyguards of the third guy next to him. I began explaining the reason for my actions when Don Pacho suddenly stopped me. He told me that I had nothing to excuse myself for and gave a warning to the two bodyguards.

"If you ever pull a stunt like this and pull a gun on one of my men, I will have both of you killed along with your families," Don Pacho threatened.

"Gus, I should've done this in the meeting, but I want the whole organization to know who Juancho is and make it clear that if they deal with him in the future they're dealing with me," he added.

After having these two apologize to the girls and to me, we made our way back to our hotel for an after party. A few of the men from the meeting were present along with their groupies. Since it wasn't my type of party I decided that 2 a.m. was an appropriate time for me to call it a night. After all, tomorrow Don Pacho and I would be making the drive to Bottrop to the Brabus Headquarters and later to the Bayern/Dortmund match.

I think I had already been asleep for an hour when I suddenly woke up to kissing and someone straddling me. It took me a second to realize that it wasn't a dream but it was one of the girls that had snuck into my bed. I must have been out cold because I don't remember taking off my clothes or a naked girl getting under the sheets with me. Once I got her off of me and had turned the lights on, I realized that it was the girl that I had defended earlier. She explained how she wanted to thank me and how no one had ever done anything like that for her. I said that it was my pleasure and encouraged her to only accept men who valued her.

SATURDAY OCTOBER 24TH, 2015

The rest of our stay in Germany went as previously planned. The following morning we made it out by 10 a.m. where one of Gus' men drove us to the Brabus headquarters to order the custom jet. On the way there Don Pacho made a comment on how he had a contact within Brabus and that he was getting a special deal on the jet. After our trip to Bottrop we returned to Dortmund in time to change and have dinner at an upscale German restaurant called Schurmanns Im Park about six minutes away from the stadium.

Once at the stadium we were taken to a private suite facing the famous Borussia Dortmund Yellow Wall on the south end of the field. Most of the faces that I had seen at the meeting the previous night were present including the two gentlemen whose butts I kicked. Their boss, a man named Dimitri Apalkov, is a self-made billionaire who made the bulk of his money from an oil conglomerate in Russia. He surprised me when he approached me to apologize for his men's behavior the previous night.

Unlike the previous night, this was a social get-together and it was treated as such by all the attendees. During the two hour match I was approached by every single important individual there and welcomed into the organization. Don Pacho wasn't kidding when he ordered that everyone know my name or who I was. This was my second taste of power since most of these men were billionaires and they were the ones introducing themselves to me. I liked it.

On Sunday, our trip's second leg led us to Barcelona where we had a similar meeting with fewer individuals. The morning meeting took place in a mansion owned by a Colombian associate of Don Pacho who was not able to make the Germany meeting. He owned several nightclubs, bars, restaurants, real estate agencies and car rental companies throughout Spain and Portugal. In a similar fashion, the men in attendance gave their reports on the current numbers for Spain and Portugal. At the end of the meeting, he invited us to the Barcelona/Rayo Vallecano match later in the afternoon; it would be my first time visiting the Camp Nou. He also made a side comment about how Lionel Messi lived in the same neighborhood.

After enjoying the 2-1 Barcelona victory we were taken straight to the Barcelona-El Prat international airport. Once we were at cruising speed, I readied myself for the red eye nine-hour flight back to the US; I was more than ready to see Brooke and Christian David. It had only been four days but to me it had felt like an eternity. For one, fighting off these girls and sleeping with one eye open, but most importantly for the type of information that I had been exposed to during both meetings. It was definitely a lot to take in for a novice drug trafficker. I might have to update my LinkedIn page to Drug Trafficker in Training.

I debated whether going to sleep or just staying up since we would be landing in Miami today in the late afternoon with the time change. I decided to send a quick Whatsapp message to Brooke to let her know that we were on our way back home. She responded quickly telling me that they had just had lunch at The Cheesecake Factory in CocoWalk. Brooke, my sister-in-law and Christian David decided to have a pool day at our new mansion before lunch time. I replied that once I was back we would have to set a date to move into our new home. Halloween was at the end of this week and I don't think that we could realistically get ourselves in moving mode by then. I did want to be settled in before I made my first trip for Don Pacho. Like I had told the boss, I had set a tentative date sometime during the first week of November to make the trip down to Colombia for the pick-up of the first $600 million. Lastly, I asked Brooke how she was doing this time around with the second pregnancy, she answered that the nausea seemed to be worse than with Christian David. I thanked her for being so tough and for being such a great mother and wife.

Since it appeared that I would be staying up I decided to work a little before turning on a movie. One of the emails I sent was to the secretary that had been assigned to me and I CC'd the operations team about getting an appointment set with the management team over at the Wells Fargo building in downtown Miami. Don Pacho wanted to have a contract signed and everyone moved into the new office building by the end of the year. I asked her to get me an appointment for either Thursday or Friday of this week and to coordinate the trip out there.

We landed in Miami a little after 5 p.m. Before dropping me off at home, I asked my driver to make a quick stop to get some flowers for Brooke and some gummy worms for Christian David. If I had to list three things that my little man has learned from me in his short life it would definitely have to be his love for Batman, the Beautiful Game and endless gummy worms.

We stopped at Avant-Gardens on 72nd Avenue and 40th street. I've been getting flowers for Brooke there since we first arrived in Florida. I tend to stick with things for a long time especially if I love the product or business; call it loyalty or laziness to look elsewhere.

At home Brooke had cooked one of my favorites for dinner, Chicken Marsala. It was actually a recipe that I first fell in love with thanks to my mother-in-law but now it was part of Brooke's short list of specialties. We had a wonderful dinner despite being overly tired from the trip. Brooke asked me the usual questions about the trip including why I hadn't brought any German chocolate for my pregnant wife.

For obvious reasons I had to give her the edited version for most of the events that went down. Not because I wanted to keep things from

Brooke, but mainly because I didn't see the need to talk about it in front of my sister-in-law.

After putting Christian David down for the night, Brooke gave me the 'Alright, let's talk about what really happened' look. This time I decided to include a little more information than I did at the dinner table, especially since the magnitude of my involvement in all of this would be greater than I expected initially. She listened intently to every word that came out of my mouth for about an hour without a word from her. When she finally spoke, the first comment was surprisingly not about what I thought it was going to be, but rather my several run-ins with the girls. After reassuring her that nothing else had happened with the girls the one question I dreaded the most finally came.

"So Juan, are you still planning on walking away after the 60 trips are completed?" she asked in an inquisitive tone.

Would I? That seemed to be the million dollar question, or based on what Don Pacho had said the billion dollar question. I had a clear understanding and plan on how I was going to complete the assignment, especially after he presented the opportunity to me. However, now I'm not entirely sure on how I'm going to proceed. I definitely can't make a decision right now; I have to give it some thought. To appease Brooke I gave her the best answer I could come up with on the spot.

"Yeah, the 60 trips," I answered non-convincingly "and that's it."

"I hope so Juan," she replied. "I didn't marry a drug trafficker or mobster."

"Just so we're clear on one thing, our marriage and family depends on your decision," she added.

"I know princess, I understand," I answered.

After dealing with the jet-lag and wrestling with a busy mind I finally got some needed sleep. At around 4 a.m. I was woken up by Brooke asking me to go check on Christian David, the poor little guy woke up crying; these night terrors are ridiculous. I closed my eyes and held him in my arms while sitting in the rocker. With each of Christian David's sighs I went deeper and deeper into sleep. The next thing I saw was a red balloon floating at eye level in the middle of a white room. I looked around me and couldn't see a door or window. The balloon was not tied down to anything and hovered in front of me. I extended my hand as an attempt to touch the balloon but I stopped myself when I noticed that I was dressed in a black suit with black everything, shirt, tie, socks and shoes.

I raised my eyes to the balloon again and as I had attempted before I stretched my hand forward to touch it. As I palmed the balloon I noticed that something was directly on the other side of it. As I turned the balloon around my heart began to race. When I saw what it was I immediately jumped back, it was a black scorpion climbing until it made its way to the top of the balloon. My initial feeling of fear quickly turned into a feeling of uneasiness as I began to worry that it would pop the balloon with its stinger. It stared into my eyes while inching its stinger closer and closer to the balloon, teasing me. I pleaded with it to stop and it did. I felt the need to thank him so I extended my hand again to touch him but as I got within an inch it suddenly shot its stinger at the balloon causing an explosion that jolted me awake.

I noticed that Christian David was no longer in my arms and I was covered

with a blanket. Brooke must have snuck in after I didn't come back to bed.

The boy was still asleep in his own bed so I tip-toed my way out of his

room. I glanced at my phone and it was already 9 a.m.

MONDAY OCTOBER 26TH, 2015 – MIAMI, FL

I wanted to get a quick workout in before breakfast so I headed

downstairs. I also felt the need to think, to give myself time to slow down

and really meditate on what all these dreams meant. I've never been

much of a dreamer nor cared much for the meaning of dreams that I've

had in the past. However, there may be a connection with the decisions

that I have been making, whether that be good or bad, in my life thus far.

After my workout I headed upstairs to have breakfast with the family.

Brooke asked me if I'd want to join her at her doctor's appointment today

especially if I had time to sneak out in the afternoon for about an hour. I

definitely wanted to be part of the whole thing so I immediately agreed to

be there.

On my way to work I made a quick stop at the Dadeland mall. Last time I was here with Brooke, I noticed a new restaurant in the food court with killer Colombian and Venezuelan food. It's called Panpaya Latin Grill; their menu includes some random Japanese sweets. I'm a big fan of their Boba drinks. While paying for my drink I received a call from my secretary. She said that the management team from the Wells Fargo building had returned her call and asked if we could meet with them earlier in the week, preferably tomorrow or Wednesday. I hadn't set any meetings for this week on purpose because I wanted to focus on next week's first pick-up, so I didn't mind. This change in plans would give us the opportunity to move into the new house before I left.

At the office I had my secretary get in contact with the moving and residential Real Estate companies owned by Don Pacho. Brooke and I had decided during breakfast this morning to list our condo for sale completely furnished. For one, it would make the moving process a lot less stressful and second, our mansion was already fully furnished with much more expensive furniture. It's a win-win.

Before I headed out the office to Brooke's appointment I had to sit in a webinar for a new corporate wide system that we'll be adding; it will facilitate the way for all of Don Pacho's companies to work with each other by allowing corporate employees to view and receive notifications about reports, deadlines and updates. Since the appointment at the Doctor's office was at 3:30 p.m. and the webinar kept dragging along, I decided to step out once I asked my secretary to keep good notes.

On my way to the appointment I was a running a little late and conveniently enough traffic was terrible so I decided to take the long way around to South Miami Hospital on 62nd Avenue. Traffic was moving faster even though I still had a genius tailgating me in a dark navy SUV. I thought I had left stupid drivers back in Utah, not so. I quickly glanced at the navigation and noticed that I was only a couple of blocks away. When I looked up I had to slam my breaks because now the fool in front of me was slowing down.

"What the hell buddy?" I slammed my hand on the steering wheel. "No one is in front of you!"

I immediately realized that it was a similar SUV and both were blocking me in. The one behind me turned on his cop lights so I pulled over. Now what? I would've been on time had it not been for this.

"Good afternoon officer, was I....?" I was interrupted halfway.

"Detective," He clarified.

"I'm sorry Detective; I don't think I was speeding," I said.

"Sir, I need you to step out of the vehicle," he ordered.

"Woah, why is that detective?" I asked bemused. "What did I do wrong?"

"Sir, we're conducting random check-ups in the area," he answered.

"Excuse me, check-ups for what?" I asked as three men wearing DEA vests surrounded my car.

"Narcotics," he said.

"Okay, but why am I the only one being stopped right now?" I asked as I climbed out of the Tumbler.

"I'm the only one pulled over," I added.

Without a word they continued to look around in my truck for a couple of minutes and just like that they jumped in their SUVs and drove away.

Alright, so that's how these bastards roll then? I guess it was just a matter of time for me to be on the DEA's radar again.

I finally made it to the hospital were Brooke was already being seen by our Doctor.

"Juan, what happened?" she asked.

"I'm sorry princess; I got pulled over a couple of blocks from here," I explained leaving out the rest of the details. No need to spoil her day. I do need to talk with Don Pacho though.

"Did I miss the ultrasound?" I asked the Doctor as I pulled a chair next to the bed.

"You didn't, just in time." She chuckled as she prepared the gel for the ultrasound.

Our baby boy, Rocky, looked great and everything was moving forward as expected for our due date on March 18th, 2016. I should be done with the 60 pick-ups by the time our boy is here. On our way out Brooke told me that she had made it a tradition to get a healthy drink from Sun Juice Smoothie & Juice bar a couple of blocks from the hospital after each of these appointments.

"So Juan, March 18th," Brooke took a sip from her kale, spinach and green apple drink. "Where do you see us in five months?"

"Where do I see us?" I asked unsure of her question. "I see us welcoming our beautiful baby boy."

"I meant our situation," she replied. "Will you be done with those 60 trips?"

"I don't want us to be dealing with that when the baby comes," she added.

"I was just thinking about that princess," I answered. "I'll be done by that date and that's it, I promise."

The reality of the situation is that I'm torn, on one end I should just collect the full amount and that's it; no need to be greedy. But on the other, I am curious as to how much money Don Pacho is referring to that I can earn if I decide to continue working with him in that capacity. Well, no need to stress out about making a decision right away.

Once Brooke and I went our separate ways I made a quick phone call to Don Pacho. I didn't want to be too specific about my run-in with the DEA over the phone with him so I just said I wanted to discuss something with him. I guess I was now a little paranoid that the DEA might be tapping my phone.

He asked me to head over to his place right away so we could chat. After the 30 minute drive through late afternoon traffic I finally made it to Don Pacho's humble abode, Palazzo Napoli. He welcomed me in to his formal dining room as he made a comment on how he didn't get to use it as much as he wanted to.

"Juancho, I know you don't drink but I just had the help open a $5,200 wine bottle," he said. "I just got a case in straight from the Côte de Nuits in France."

"Not even a sip?" he offered.

"Thank you Don Pacho, I'll pass but I will have an Italian soda if you have any," I replied.

The kitchen staff proceeded to serve us a full three-course meal. I've never had duck before. After our lavish dessert, Don Pacho asked me what I wanted to talk about. I began explaining my earlier run-in with the DEA and noted that I didn't think it was the first time it had happened. I thought to myself how perfect the situation was right now to get an answer about his possible involvement in the condo fire, but how do you bring up something like that?

I reminded him about the man who had been spying on me from across the street and the unusual fire that was started later that night. I also explained what the pizza delivery boy had told me about his several deliveries to that unit and how they were DEA agents. I was contemplating on the words that I was going to use for my question when his answer caught me by surprise.

"I know," he said with conviction as he lit up a Cuban cigar.

"Excuse me Don Pacho?" I asked.

"I said I know," he clarified. "Those men were surveilling you as a way to get to me."

"After I left your place that day I had some of my men look into it," he added.

Despite having a hunch about it this whole time his admission to being involved in the fire still hit me like a cold bucket of water. I was left completely speechless and I consciously made the effort to keep a neutral reaction, whatever that looks like. But even though I tried to play it cool, he still could read me.

"Juancho, I don't want you to worry about this or anything else," he explained. "I think I've had a slight hunch that you knew or at least suspected that I was involved in the fire."

"However, you've stuck with me showing your loyalty to me," he added.

He emphasized my importance to him and the whole organization, especially now that I was his second in command. According to him loyalty is an attribute that does not have a price meaning that he is willing to pay me half a billion dollars or more if necessary to have me on his side. I'm beginning to see how really deep I am in all of this.

He went on to explain that several organizations including the DEA, FBI and Miami Police Department have been surveilling or at least trying to pin anything on him for the last few years. He said that it began after the DEA was able to seize a rather small shipment from one of his cargo ships coming from Colombia. He was able to clear himself from any wrong doing meaning that he either paid someone off or had someone else take the heat for it.

He concluded his little monologue by adding yet more wood to the fire. At first I thought I had understood his general philosophy about how money could give an individual a great amount of power. I believed I had tasted some of that power but it seems that I haven't fully understood the magnitude of that power that he's referring to.

"Juancho, if I was to ask right now who the richest man in the world is today, who would you say that is?" he asked.

"Well, according to Forbes it's between Bill Gates and Carlos Slim," I replied.

"How much does Forbes say each of them is worth at this time?" he asked again.

"I think it's somewhere between $75-80 billion each." I answered.

"Juancho, let me tell you something that will make you the only other person to know this besides myself," he said.

"When you complete the 60 pick-ups and you've collected your 1% as payment for the work performed, my personal net worth will surpass the $100 billion mark," he added.

He explained that on paper he only had a net worth of $25 billion, however, he had $40 billion that was not public and was currently under other aliases in various international accounts. With the added chunk of $36 billion minus my commission that fortune would make him the richest man alive. I think that actually makes sense, after his simulated death in 1993 he continued to build his wealth for the last two decades and it will only continue to grow for who knows how many years.

"If you stick with me in the long run my friend, I promise I will make you the second richest man in the world." He proposed.

The drive back home was really tough with my mind going all over the place. I tried playing every possible different scenario with the possible outcome based on the variety of decisions I could make once the 60 pick-ups were complete. The once clear black and white options for me were becoming a lot more grayish as time went on. Don Pacho was definitely not making it any easier to walk away from this with all the never ending offers.

In a blink of an eye I was already pulling into our building not knowing how I made the 30-minute drive in one piece. Brooke's note on the fridge said that she had to fill in for a last minute Hip Hop class and had to take Christian David with her. Her sister had started a part-time job today at a clothing store in Dadeland Mall.

With the residuals of jet lag still kicking my butt I decided to call it a night. I must have been in bed five minutes when my phone lit up the dark room with an incoming text. I had totally forgotten that some of the Guatemalan guys from the Kendall carwash that I supervised had invited me to join their indoor soccer team. The first game was tonight at 8:45; it was 8:30 right now. I changed and texted Brooke on my way to the game. Despite being overly tired, it was a great way to end the night and get my mind off of work or the pressures of any impending life-changing decisions.

TUESDAY OCTOBER 27TH, 2015

This morning I got up to a call from my secretary telling me that the movers wanted to know when we were planning to move. I told her that we wanted to get it done on Thursday and to plan on a midsize truck since no furniture would be coming along with us. She reminded me of today's meeting with the people of the Wells Fargo building and asked me if I would be driving separately or together with the operations team. The operations department consisted of three very attractive girls in their mid to late 20's; just how Don Pacho liked them. I told her that we could carpool in my truck.

After lunch I met up with the girls in the office and headed to downtown Miami. We joined the Wells Fargo management team in the lobby and we briefly discussed what floors were available. Knowing Don Pacho I didn't hesitate to pick the last three floors for the walk-through; it would definitely make Don Pacho happy knowing that he could use his helicopter more often. We made our way up to floors 45, 46 and 47 while we were told about our multi-billion dollar neighbors should we decide to sign on the dotted line today. My mind drifted a little on how Don Pacho was worth more than all of these companies combined and then some.

It was no surprise that the views and quality of this building were going to be out of this world; reason why I didn't hesitate on telling the girls to get the contract done right away. While that was being done I asked one of the Wells Fargo people if I could take a look at the roof. To my surprise the roof did not look anything like the dream I had a few weeks ago, for one the dream included a helipad which the building didn't have. We were in the process of discussing the reason why the building didn't have one when I heard Don Pacho's voice behind me.

"We'll simply have to throw some money at the building and get it done," he chuckled as the rest of the group joined us.

"What would it cost to add a helipad to this rooftop?" he asked our hosts.

We were told that they had looked into it a few years back but the cost was not worth the addition. According to them none of the current tenants had a need for it. That statement could only encourage Don Pacho into doing it since he always makes sure that people know that he's the extravagant billionaire in the room. We finished discussing the details associated with the addition noting that money wasn't an issue and we ended the meeting with a signed ten year contract starting on November 9.

Once in the lobby we thanked our hosts and parted ways. Don Pacho took a minute to tell us that he was open to the possibility of buying this building someday in the future and asked the girls to passively look into it. Don Pacho likes the idea of owning a building that adjoins the JW Marriott Marquis Hotel; one of two in the world after Dubai's. I wouldn't be surprised if he wanted to buy both hotels as part of the same package deal; the man sees a price on everything and doesn't accept No for an answer.

"Juancho, do you have any plans for Halloween with the family?" he asked while the valet brought the Tumbler out from the underground parking.

"We'll be settled in the new house by Saturday so I thought that trick-or-treating around the new neighborhood would be a great way to meet the neighbors," I replied.

"Why don't you bring the family over to Palazzo Napoli this Friday?" he offered. "I'm having human resources send an email-invite today to all employees and their families in South Florida to my Halloween party."

"We'll have a magician, a haunted house, a giant movie screen outside, food and treats." He added just as the valet pulled up.

I told him to count us in for the party and asked if we should bring anything. I asked only because I know that Brooke will ask me if I offered; Don Pacho goes all out at these things. We would be taking Christian David trick-or-treating on Saturday so I think he'll have a blast at the party with other kids.

Once I dropped off the girls at the office I headed home a little early. Brooke and I wanted to go on a last minute date since my sister-in-law was going to be off tonight. We also wanted to celebrate the sale of our condo today. It appears that our realtor had done a walk-through earlier today and the couple ended up making a full offer before I even got home. We decided to celebrate the sale and the move to the new house by trying a new place for dinner. We headed over to our new neighborhood, Coconut Grove, to enjoy some Latin American cuisine at Jaguar Ceviche Spoon Bar & Latam Grill on CocoWalk.

Wednesday was spent in its entirety getting ready for the move and cleaning the condo. I did get a call from my dad in the late afternoon that went on for a couple of hours. He told me that he was getting ready to fly to Colombia tomorrow morning because my grandma was on her deathbed and the doctor had given her a week at most. I offered to get him and my mom on a chartered jet straight to Colombia but it would leave Friday; he declined and said that he had already purchased the tickets.

Thursday was moving day and it went smoother than I planned. The idea of moving residences with an expectant mother and an active three-year-old could only make things worse; I'm glad we decided to sell the condo fully furnished. The moving truck showed up at 10 a.m. and we were fully moved into our newly furnished home by 3 p.m.; it must be the easiest and fastest move I've seen in my life.

We hadn't finished emptying the few boxes that did make it over when Christian David was already wearing his swim trunks and asking for the pool. Our relaxing moving day ended with a quiet evening pool side and delivered pizza from Anthony's.

FRIDAY OCTOBER 30TH, 2015

This morning I walked into a rather hectic office. Don Pacho wanted to begin the move into the new building on Monday, luckily for me I would be at 33,000 feet over the Caribbean going to the first pick-up. All office and carwash personnel were allowed to head home at 3:30 p.m. in preparation for the party tonight. As a side note, even though only South Florida employees would be making the party, Don Pacho wanted all employees companywide to have a short day.

"Mr. Arias, just a reminder to turn off your computer before you head out today," my secretary reminded me from the door way. "We're starting the move at 8 a.m. on Monday."

"What did I say the other day, call me Juan," I responded as I looked away from a Google Earth map of Colombia. When Don Pacho gave me the location of the first five pick-ups, he listed them as individual trips. However, I don't see why I couldn't get all five done in one trip. That will be a nice $30 million payday once I get back.

Driving up Don Pacho's house was a sight to behold; the whole property was a massive Halloween production surpassing some local haunted houses. His mini-airstrip of a driveway was filled with cars while the main road was bumper to bumper traffic with people taking pictures of the property. As we walked through the crowd towards the back of the house

I was surprised not to see his usual female posse wearing revealing clothes. This was actually a family friendly party focusing on the children.

"Welcome vampires, ghosts, ninjas and superheroes!" Don Pacho said from the stage with the theater size screen. "Welcome to the best Halloween party in Southern Florida, please enjoy the grounds and don't forget to enter your name for the $5,000 best costume contest."

"We'll be having the Halloween costume contest at 7 p.m. since we know there are early bed times for some of you," he added.

I was able to get a virgin Piña Colada for Brooke while she made herself a plate at one of the many food tables. Christian David on the other hand was way too over-stimulated by everything and we couldn't get him to eat.

"Just go with him, he won't eat anything right now," Brooke said. "I'll be fine; I'll just watch the movie."

It only took him about 20 minutes of jumping from game to game until finally finding a favorite in the foam pit. While waiting I felt an arm around me; Don Pacho smoking his usual cigar and with a grin on his face.

"Juancho, are you excited for next week?" Don Pacho asked. "Because if you're not I am."

"Do you have any last minute questions?" he added.

"I do, but shouldn't we go somewhere else to talk?" I asked thinking that this topic was better to discuss in private.

"Nah, it's loud and nobody can hear us," he responded.

"What's on your mind my friend?" he asked.

"Well Don Pacho, since the first five pick-ups are all in Colombia, can I just do all of them in one trip?" I asked.

"Are you sure you want to do all five?" he asked. "That would take a week or possibly longer."

"I initially planned on single trips because I didn't want to keep you away from your family for too long," he explained.

"Are you sure you want to leave Brooke for that long?" he questioned.

"I think it would be ideal to get as many done as possible before the baby is born," I said.

"Alright Juancho, if that's what you prefer, then we'll do it like that," he smiled while patting me on the back. "I'll have to get those $30 million from under the mattress for you."

Lastly Don Pacho said that there would be a packet with instructions and a GPS waiting for me in the jet on Monday. He wished me good luck and stepped away to take a call.

Christian David and I helped ourselves to some monster ice cream cones before joining Brooke at our table.

"So, what were you talking about with your boss?" asked Brooke.

"We were just talking about the final details for next week's pick-ups," I replied as I cleaned up Batman's chocolate covered face.

"Pick-ups? I thought it was going to be a single pick-up?" she asked.

"I thought so initially, but it'll be all five pick-ups for this trip to Colombia," I answered.

"For how long will you be leaving your pregnant wife and toddler alone?" she asked annoyed.

"I believe two weeks but most likely less," I replied trying to sugar coat my answer and hopefully surprise her by returning earlier than expected.

Despite Brooke not being thrilled at my upcoming long absence I reminded her that once I was back we would be $30 million richer. I told her that one of the things on my to-do list after payday was to buy her dance studio which seemed to soften the harsh news a bit. In addition I wanted to build a custom home on an empty half-acre lot that Brooke's parents have had for the last eight years back in Utah. Upon completion my plan would be to sell it and split the earnings two ways. The list of pending investments was long but it mostly consisted of various projects that I needed capital for in the past but I didn't have. I want to leave my children their own little business empire.

The best Halloween party in South Florida ended right at 9 p.m.; Don Pacho wasn't kidding about ending in time for early bed times. Brooke got second runner-up in the adult's costume division with my secretary taking first place and the $5,000 prize for her Harley Quinn costume. Christian David was hopped up in sugar and most likely would not be going to bed for a while. Lastly, my imminent week-long getaway to Colombia where I would return a multi-millionaire was becoming more and more real now.

Our Saturday was pretty relaxed; it consisted of enjoying our new home and eating an unhealthy amount of Halloween candy from the party. My next thought might have been product of ingesting too much sugar but I was inspired to begin yet another new project once I was back from abroad. We would have the tennis court taken out and replaced with a covered indoor soccer field with clear walls for extra natural light. I did a quick search online about the cost of a turf field and depending on the measurements I was looking at somewhere between $65K and $75K. Meanwhile, Brooke and her sister made a quick trip to the store to get some more groceries since we only bought the essentials yesterday. Christian David and I were able to try out our new 20-seat home theater by watching one of his favorites, Big Hero 6, for the millionth time in the last couple of months.

We had an exceptional dinner made by the girls at 5 p.m. and by 6 p.m. we were out the door trick-or-treating on our street. Despite being 20 weeks pregnant Brooke decided to join us so she could also meet the neighbors. The list is somewhat long but our street has a couple of celebrities, some high-profile executives, a famous novelist, a popular Telemundo TV anchor, the City Mayor and funny enough, the Director of the DEA living a couple of houses down from us. He wasn't home so we'll have to befriend him and his family by sending a plate of Arepas or poisoned cookies sometime in the near future. Then again, he already attempted to make first contact with me with two of his surveillance teams in the past few weeks.

Sunday was an even more relaxed day than yesterday. I woke up just in time to watch Real Madrid and Barcelona face off in this year's first Clasico on my own movie screen; the best way to watch this game other than being there in person. The rest of the family woke up at noon so by the time we were ready to eat we decided to make a huge late brunch or linner if that's the correct term. The unexpected event of the day was the Mayor's visit in the evening accompanied by his wife and two grandkids. They live kitty corner to us in an even bigger mansion. We had a great chat about our professions and about our families. He even invited us to join them in their home in two weeks for the neighborhood's monthly Meet & Greet. Being the new family in the block we would be spotlighted and welcomed into the neighborhood by everyone. I guess this would be my chance to meet the head of the DEA face to face and start my long-term "friendly" courtship; Don Pacho will have a laugh when he hears this.

MONDAY NOVEMBER 2ND, 2015

The big day was here; it began with a good workout followed by the execution of my culinary skills in the kitchen with a good breakfast. With our recent lifestyle change I suggested that we should really consider getting a cook. We could have him or her take care of lunch and dinner while we handled breakfast. In addition, we would also need to look into a trustworthy maid service and landscaping company. I've never been a fan of doing yard work anyways and I'm a firm believer that if you want something well done you shouldn't skimp on the job that a professional can do.

One of Don Pacho's drivers picked me up right at 10 a.m. Upon boarding the jet I was given a sealed manila folder with the instructions inside and a small size box. Once we were in the air heading to Colombia I noticed that the box not only had the GPS that I would be using this whole week but also a brand new satellite phone. I spent a good hour and a half getting familiar with Don Pacho's instructions and itinerary.

Upon touching down in Medellin I would be staying for a day at the Dann Carlton Medellin Hotel in the upscale neighborhood of El Poblado. Don Pacho said that he wanted me to relax, have fun and get in the mindset needed to begin the heavy work week on Tuesday morning. The next day I would check out early and meet up with the excavation team. The excavation teams would have between 50 and 70 men working to get a total of 50 drums at each location totaling 250 drums. Once the first pick-up was complete we would head back to the airport where the barrels would be loaded into a C-5 Galaxy cargo plane. Don Pacho mentioned that just for this trip we would be using this behemoth; the plane we would be using on a regular basis would be a C-130J Super Hercules. From Medellin we would fly to the next pick-up in Buenaventura where I would spend the night on board the plane. According to Don Pacho's notes, Buenaventura's airport wasn't built for a plane this size therefore the landing, and especially the take-off, would be a tricky one which explains why Buenaventura needs to be one of the first pick-ups to avoid having too much additional weight.

Wednesday would be spent retrieving the drums out of this site and like the night before; we would load the plane once again and head out to

Pasto to the south near the Colombia/Ecuador border. Thursday would be spent in Pasto but due to the distance between Pasto and the next pick-up in Cucuta, Friday's pick-up might go down a little later in the day. If necessary we would possibly have to push the actual excavation to Saturday morning; that change in plans would take the completion of the operation to Sunday in the Sincelejo area.

Don Pacho apologized for the inconvenience of having to sleep in the plane but emphasized that being the second in command required certain things like keeping an eye on the whole operation including the plane once the barrels were loaded. According to him no one else knew the contents of the barrels other than me, not even the pilots. My job would be done once all barrels were loaded in the monster plane. I still didn't know the destination but apparently the pilots do.

He concluded the instructions by describing how we had paid off some high ranking officials in the Colombian military, thus giving us the luxury of having military escorts for all of the pick-ups.

I stood up to stretch a little just as one of the pilots was coming out of the cockpit.

"Mr. Arias, how's everything?" he asked as he opened a bottle of water.

"Good thanks," I replied. "Where are we right now?"

"We're passing Jamaica as we speak," he answered.

"It should be another hour to reach the Colombian coast and another 30 minutes to make Medellin," he added.

After a quick restroom break I returned to my seat and decided to take a look at my Facebook account. I specifically wanted to see if there were any updates on my grandmother's condition. A cousin had posted a few pictures of the whole family including my parents the night they arrived. Depending on how things play out I was hoping I could stop in Bogota once the job was completed. I haven't been to Colombia since I was 12 when we went for a couple of weeks during the summer of '97.

We touched down in Medellin a little before 3 p.m. A Land Cruiser pulled up to the jet as the flight attendant opened the door. I was taken to the hotel where I was able to relax and focus on the job just as Don Pacho had instructed. What better way to do it that in style in one of the hotel's premium suites. The weather was amazing; according to my room's alarm clock it was in the low 70s perfect for some pool time. For dinner I was encouraged by the front desk to try the five-star revolving Tony Roma's restaurant on their top floor with stunning views of one of Colombia's major cities. Medellin has had a tremendous change in the last two decades since the Medellin Cartel was dismantled, or in other words, since Escobar changed zip codes.

TUESDAY NOVEMBER 3RD, 2015 – MEDELLIN, COLOMBIA

I slept surprisingly well considering that I usually struggle to sleep before a big event or trip. It's 8 a.m. and before I head downstairs to get some breakfast I got a quick ab workout in to get me going for the day. Last night I made sure that the coordinates for the first pick-up were in and that the satellite phone was ready; I made a quick call to Don Pacho. I made my way downstairs to get breakfast before meeting my ride at 10 a.m. This hotel is pretty impressive, I would love to bring Brooke, Christian David and also my in-laws since they always ask me if it's safe to travel to Colombia.

At 10 a.m. I was picked up by the same Land Cruiser from yesterday with two additional Land Cruisers behind us. A couple of blocks from the hotel we were met by an 18-wheeler. At this point I was asked by my driver to give him the GPS. The drive up to the pick-up location took a little past an hour as we passed a few farms and were also joined by three military jeeps.

"We're here," our driver announced through his radio to the truck and other vehicles.

As the 18-wheeler was brought around and backed up a ways, I noticed that there was a second 18-wheeler coming up the hill and heading our way.

"Are they with us?" I asked.

"Yes, it's for the workers once they're done," my driver answered as groups of men started exiting the trailer.

I lost count but it must have been between 50 and 60 men that were inside the trailer. About 20 of them were armed with assault rifles while the rest appeared to be local farmers. I was told that once the first trailer was loaded, the second trailer would serve as a shuttle to get all these workers out of here.

The workers lined up behind the second trailer which was loaded with shovels and a forklift. Don Pacho mentioned in the instructions that we would not be using any large and heavy machinery to do the jobs. In addition to having two of the three jeeps create military checkpoints; we would be doing the whole thing old school, by hand, to avoid attracting any unwanted attention to ourselves.

With the GPS in hand I paired up the latitude and longitude coordinates which took us behind a small grove of trees and just like that the large group of men began the excavation efforts. Within three hours the men had dug a 20X20 hole and about 10-15 feet deep. It was surreal standing over the hole and seeing the blue air-tight drums containing $600 million in cash. Two whole decades of buried treasure with 59 more still to go. The drums were aligned and stacked on top of each other in five rows of five columns totaling 50 drums. They were also tied to each other with a steel cable that had to be cut for the forklift to do its job. It only took two additional hours to get the drums out, loaded in the truck and the hole covered.

The second trailer was loaded with the workers and out of our sight within minutes. We proceeded to make our way to the airport where the plane was already waiting for us. As we pulled up to the gates at the north end of the airport our driver pulled out a brown paper bag which I assume was money for the security guards. Once we were past the gates we drove to the other side of a warehouse where a FedEX plane was parked and being loaded. Next to it was our monster cargo plane that looked three times the size of any commercial airliner and had been strategically branded as a Red Cross plane; interesting decoy approach.

While the drums were unloaded, saran wrapped and placed on pallets, I was approached by four men who introduced themselves as the C-5's crew. They spoke Spanish with German accents; however they preferred to carry the conversation in English. These guys must be part of Gus' crew back in Germany.

I was given a quick tour of the inside of the plane and shown where I would be sleeping for the rest of the trip. I was also given some details about the aircraft such as weight capacity, fueling times and how it was a recently retired US army plane when Don Pacho came across the opportunity to buy it.

After checking off the first 50 drums on board we took off a little after sunset heading to our second location in Buenaventura. I was invited into the cockpit to discuss or rather confirm the schedule for the following day. As instructed per Don Pacho I advised them that we would spend the night in the plane and meet the excavation team in the morning at 8 a.m.

We made it to Buenaventura in just 45 minutes in a plane that was four times the size of the only building here. Tomorrow we will witness whether a plane this size can really defy the law of gravity and take off from a runway that even lacks the width necessary to turn around.

As I prepared my cot for the night, one of the pilots opened the side door and three men driving in a military Jeep handed us a few bags of food. The whole transfer was made in complete silence from both parties. Thus far there has not been any socializing of any kind, not since I left the hotel yesterday morning. The few times we've exchanged words were just to ask single phrase questions and make job related comments. It's good to see that everyone is focused on the job and completing the pick-ups as fast as possible.

Despite not taking part in the physical aspect of the excavation I was physically and mentally exhausted. I glanced at my watch and it was 10:15 p.m. meaning that I could easily pull a 9 to 10 hour night's sleep. I set my alarm at 7:15 a.m. which would give me enough time to get ready for yet another long day; however, my body decided otherwise and was completely awake at 4 a.m. None of the crew members seemed to be awake yet so I decided to send a quick message to Brooke and Christian David – *'Good morning, I love you guys. We're in Buenaventura (2nd location, Pacific coast). Everything is well and on schedule. I'll send another message tonight once we make it to Pasto. Have a great day guys.'*

WEDNESDAY NOVEMBER 4TH, 2015 – BUENAVENTURA, COLOMBIA

To kill some time I decided to do a little workout but with the lack of resources I found myself being pretty creative. On the opposite side of my cot I saw a steel ladder that was part of the plane's structural body and I was able to use it for pull-ups. I used some large heavy duty chains which I assume are used for strapping down large cargo, and used them as added weight for push-ups and squats. I must have lost track of time because the next thing I heard was the sound of a semi's horn. It was 8 a.m. and my alarm never went off.

We followed the same procedure from our first pick-up near Medellin, only this time our caravan had two semi-trucks right from the beginning with five Jeeps, three of which were military. I handed the GPS with the entered coordinates to my driver and we headed south west away from the airport. After taking a 10-minute drive across a bridge over the Danubio River and zigzagging through some residential areas we ended up alongside the same river in a less densely-vegetated area.

Both trucks were turned around, backed up and parked side by side as a way to minimize the time spent doing the job. The first trailer's doors were opened and out came a new crew of workers; each was handed a shovel as I made my way to the exact point where we would begin the excavation. As opposed to our first pick-up, this time we had a little less than 50 men, taking into account that a fourth of that number are here purely for fire power and not digging duty. In similar fashion the excavation revealed the 50 sealed drums connected to each other with a steel cable, another day another $600 million. After a few hours work we were once again at the mini-airport transferring the load to the plane. Now it was time to see if this monster could take off from this runway carrying a total of $1.2 billion in cash. To get additional room for take-off we backed up past the beginning of the runway and into the dirt. I was told that the C-5 Galaxy would usually require a minimum of 5,000 feet at take-off, but after the crew measured the runway we would have to do the same with only 4,500 feet or a fiery grave in the Danubio River.

With all four turbofan engines roaring at full power and some nervy moments, we were finally airborne skimming over the trees and river. The next 45 minute leg would take us south to Pasto near the Colombia/Ecuador border. We would be landing in Pasto's second and much smaller airport in the outskirts of the city. The coordinates for this pick-up showed a 30-minute drive west of the airport to a small town called Criollos where Don Pacho owned 100+ acres of farm land.

Upon touching down in Pasto we had a minor scare due to the heavy Andean rain in the area. Despite the runway being longer than Buenaventura's, it seemed for a moment that we would not stop in time before face planting into the hillside. After debating for a moment if I should change my underwear we parked on an abandoned second runway where a military truck was already there with food for us. If this rain continues through the night, the whole excavation experience tomorrow will definitely be one to remember. Looking at the bright side, at this time tomorrow night we will be more than halfway done and closer to hitting the $2 billion mark, that's $20 million for moi. We also have a longer runway so I think it'll be a good day tomorrow.

I sent a quick message to Brooke checking in for the day and called it a night.

THURSDAY NOVEMBER 5TH, 2015 – PASTO, COLOMBIA

Just as the previous couple of days we began work at an early hour. This time the only military escort that would accompany us through the day was the truck with soldiers for the road blocks. I jumped in one of the three jeeps leading the way to our next pick-up site 30 minutes away. Luckily the rain had ceased overnight leaving us with very muddy conditions; I'm glad I'm not doing the digging.

Today's dig took longer than the others but it got done which is what really matters. We also had to deal with one of the semi's getting stuck in the mud; luckily the other semi and the army truck got it out in time to make it back to the airport right after nightfall. In a blink of an eye we were airborne once again heading to Cucuta near the Colombia/Venezuela border. I decided to take a quick look at the next pick-up's coordinates in the GPS; the actual site is a short 20-minute drive north east along the border past a small town called Santa Cecilia.

We made it to my late Grandfather's hometown of Cucuta at 3 a.m. I'm definitely exhausted but we'll keep the current schedule and keep moving forward with the second to last pick-up. The way I see it minor things like exhaustion or lack of sleep are not worth slowing down the momentum; momentum is money. One thing for sure is that this is the first and last time I'll be doing multiple pick-ups in one trip.

FRIDAY NOVEMBER 6TH, 2015 – CUCUTA, COLOMBIA

The workday moved smoothly as we were escorted to and from the site by a military convoy once again. The next 50 drums taking us up to $2.4 billion were loaded and ready for take-off. Once in the air I made a comment to my German friends about how we might have overdone it with the fire power. They quickly replied that the fire power was mainly planned with our last destination in mind; I guess Don Pacho forgot or decided to leave that part out of the packet.

After the end of Escobar and the Medellin cartel in 1993, the Cali cartel was able to operate as the new leader in the drug trafficking world. Two short years later, the Orejuela brothers were taken down by the authorities which led to the birth of the Norte del Valle cartel which at one time was led by a former cop gone bad, Wilber Varela. I guess the man learned the ins and outs of the game from his end and saw a more lucrative career until he was murdered by his own men in 2008. Since then the quest for power and leadership in this industry has splintered into various organizations with remnants of the old cartels as well as paramilitary groups wanting a piece of the pie.

They emphasized how we were a global organization and did not want to associate with lesser groups in Colombia or Mexico. As a global and separate entity we handled a world market rather than just the US market. All this led to beefing up our fire power in case we ran into any of these groups demanding to know what we were doing on their turf.

SATURDAY NOVEMBER 7TH, 2016 – SINCELEJO, COLOMBIA

Not knowing exactly what the day in Sincelejo would bring us, I decided to send a quick message to Brooke and Christian David. I wanted to tell them how much I loved them while not trying to sound worried; especially avoiding to cause any worry to the expectant mother. Our new escort today included an armed military helicopter, a truck full of soldiers, the two semis and our Land Cruiser. We were ready to make this the fastest pick-up yet.

The excavation moved quickly and efficiently; even loading the barrels in the trailer in record time. As we were wrapping up the operation, we received a radio call from the second truck carrying the workers down the small canyon.

"Manada de lobos sueltos!" shouted the driver which literally means "Loose pack of wolves".

"What does that mean?" I asked Humberto, my driver.

"It means that we have company coming our way," he answered as he relayed the information to everyone via his radio.

Our caravan quickly came to a stop so both the soldiers and our 20 heavily armed men could get out. They all seemed to be getting ready for something big. I'm not going to lie, my heart started racing a little bit not knowing what to expect. Humberto must have seen my worried look because he said that all of our vehicles including the semi were bullet proof and that we also had the upper hand with the helicopter.

In a matter of minutes we could see the caravan heading up the hill towards us. As they approached I could see about a half dozen Hummers and a truck full of men right behind them. Once they reached us, they came to a complete stop blocking our way. About 50 or so men exited all the vehicles; all of them carrying assault rifles. We were outnumbered, but then again, we did have the helicopter.

One of the soldiers in the truck approached three men that exited the first Hummer. He spoke with them for a few minutes while pointing at our truck and up the hill a few times.

"Who are these guys?" I asked.

"I think it's The Urabeños," he replied. "It's one of two major Cartels that fight for this territory."

I had actually read about these guys, the article described them as one of the most ruthless and aggressive trafficking organizations with a large national presence all over Colombia. I noticed that our guy was shaking hands with the men as if finishing their conversation.

"I guess everything is fine." I commented to Humberto as our guy started walking back our way. He was halfway to the truck when I noticed that one of the men with a radio turned around and shot our guy in the back of the head.

"Oh, sh…" I yelled as I tried to process what I had seen but was immediately interrupted half sentence when I saw a rocket come out of nowhere and take out our helicopter from behind. A black helicopter came out of a wooded area and flew past us as an all-out battle began between both sides. Without our helicopter we were now badly outnumbered. Humberto got on the radio yelling for air support as he handed me an assault rifle. Luckily it wasn't my first time handling a weapon like this, but there was a little more pressure now than at my local Miami gun range. I rolled my window down just enough to take out my weapon when the helicopter blew up the truck full of soldiers in front of us like it was nothing.

"Air support will be here in five minutes," yelled Humberto over the noise of the bullets hitting our bullet proof SUV.

"We have to hold them until then," he added as he slammed on the gas backing us until we were behind the semi.

"Turn the truck so we can have some cover!" he radioed the truck.

While our men tried to fight back Humberto jumped in the back seat and took out a bazooka. He opened the sunroof and as he was aiming at the helicopter he was hit in the shoulder by an impossible shot. I pulled him back in, bleeding profusely as I closed the sun roof.

"You need to take out that helicopter," he gasped for air. "We don't stand a chance with it in the air."

He quickly showed me what to do and now it was up to me to blow this thing out of the sky. To make things more complicated he said we only had one shot so there was no room for error. If I tried to pull the same thing I would definitely get picked off by one of the sharp shooters and I was not going to die here today.

I radioed the truck and had the driver order half of our men to shoot at the helicopter buying me a few seconds to get a clear shot with the bazooka. My bloodied driver pulled closer to the truck so I could get out. As my men gave the chopper hell I was able to get an unobstructed shot but before I could pull the trigger the guy next to me was shot in the head from behind us; we were beginning to be surrounded and our guys were falling quickly. I was able to get in the SUV again and changed the plan. In a split second I was able to visualize what we needed to do. Humberto was unconscious but still alive despite the loss of blood; this was all up to me now.

I got him to the back seat and I jumped in the driver's seat, and put the bazooka on my lap while opening the sunroof just enough to fit the bazooka.

"Have all the men shoot at the chopper!" I yelled over the radio as I drove around the truck and floored it. This could be a suicidal plan but it had to work. As a wave of incoming bullets hit every inch of my SUV, I ducked to avoid the airbag and drove into one of the Hummers that was directly under the chopper. Despite the hard impact I was able to turn myself face up, aim and pull the trigger. In a swift motion I was able to put the Land Cruiser in reverse and slam on the gas as I heard the chopper get blown to bits. I rammed into the front of our truck not being able to see where I was going. I immediately heard a second explosion but was unable to see as my windshield was completely obliterated; our air support had arrived and blew most of the Hummers away.

In a matter of minutes the gun fire had ceased. After the dust settled, we realized that despite losing most of our men we had been able to withstand a massive attack with only a few survivors on the opposite end running away. I couldn't believe what I had just experienced. What I had seen millions of times on TV and movies had just turned into reality. I wrestled with death face to face, blowing up a helicopter in the process and I somehow made it out alive.

With my SUV completely destroyed I jumped in the truck and we made our way to the airport with a new military escort. Trying to shake of the eerie feeling of having come so close to death I pulled out my phone and there was a message from Brooke; it had a time stamp of 30 minutes ago.

'We love you and we hope you're staying safe.'

If she only knew what was going down at the time she typed the message. Back at the airport the last 50 drums were loaded in the plane coming to a total of 250 drums carrying $3 billion in cash. My 30 million dollar job was complete; the loaded C-5 Galaxy took off right before sunset.

Don Pacho's jet was already here waiting for me so we made a quick flight to Bogota. Once in the air I placed a surprise call to my parents to tell them that I was on my way there. Unfortunately, I was told that my Grandmother had passed away a couple of days ago and I would have to rush to make the funeral at least. We made it to Bogota where I was met by my parents and most of my dad's side of the family; I hadn't seen my relatives in such a long time and after having gone through some intense situations this past week, it was nice to be with family. We spent the next few hours catching up at my Grandmother's house where I had lived during a short part of my childhood.

MONDAY NOVEMBER 9TH, 2015 – BOGOTA, COLOMBIA

The funeral took place early Monday morning; it was attended by a large amount of extended family. After the funeral we headed back home to have lunch; my Grandmother would've loved to know that all her family was gathered celebrating her life instead of the usual dull and dreary funerals.

Unfortunately my time here was very limited; I had to head back home to Brooke and Christian David so I said my goodbyes promising to come back soon or better yet, bring all of them to visit us in Miami. Why not? I can definitely afford it now.

As previously planned I surprised my two loves at home while they took a dip in our pool. To my surprise they had quite a gathering with what I'm guessing are some of our neighbors, nothing better than other children peeing in my pool.

"Honey, you're home early!" said Brooke with a smile from ear to ear. "I told myself this morning that today was going to be a great day and now you show up early, I love it."

"I think you've already met a few of these ladies but let me introduce you again," Brooke added.

I was introduced to a half-dozen ladies from our neighborhood, some of them wearing some pretty intense swimsuits; plenty of high maintenance women here in attendance. The last woman I met was none other than the Director of the DEA's wife from down the street.

"Juan, this is Mallory Haight, her husband is the Director of the DEA here in Miami," Brooke said. "You remember."

"I do, very nice to see you again," I responded.

"My husband and I would love to have you and your family over for dinner sometime this week," she offered. "He really wants to meet you Juan."

I bet he does, fool.

"We'll definitely get something planned, thank you Mallory," I replied.

The pool but especially the hot tub sounded wonderful right now, so I went inside to unpack the few things I had taken with me on the trip. I played with Christian David for a bit in the pool before hitting the hot tub while feeling the intense looks from most of these cougars.

While in the hot tub I received a call from Don Pacho congratulating me for the job well done and wanting to give me my well-deserved compensation. I told him that I'd be there a little later but first I wanted to have dinner with the family. As our party guests made their way out the door Brooke made me laugh with a comment about whether I had noticed how all the women were staring at me. I knew better so I answered that I did not notice. She also told me that while I was gone she had hired a chef to do the cooking for lunches and dinners; today was his third day.

After enjoying a gourmet meal with the people I love, I took Christian David with me to Don Pacho's to collect our small fortune. I decided to take Brooke's SUV because it would definitely fit a lot more than mine. At Palazzo Napoli, Don Pacho welcomed us by having his staff offer us authentic Italian gelato imported straight from Italy; my sugar addicted kid loved it. Don Pacho had offered to pay me using wire transfers but I insisted that the first payment be made in cash; I wanted to see and hold the cash in my hands. There's something about the visual and feel of $30 million in cash in front of you, that makes all your senses come alive.

To my amazement Brooke's SUV did not have enough room for the 10 black duffle bags each carrying $3 million. I ended up having to get a mini trailer at a local U-Haul store a couple of miles away thus making it the most expensive mini trailer in the world. Back at Don Pacho's we had a brief discussion about the operation, the logistics and how it went down including the bloody battle near Sincelejo. He apologized for not being 100% clear and honest with me about the possible run-in with one of the two cartels. He mentioned that he had already been briefed about how things unfolded and how I handled myself saving the few survivors that were left.

"Juancho, not that I ever doubted your abilities or loyalty, but you have definitely outdone yourself," Don Pacho said. "The only thing that I can do to show you a portion of my amazement and appreciation for you is to increase your take to two percent for the remainder of the jobs."

"This would almost double the initial take from $360 million to $690 million," he noted.

Despite being in the presence of death, by far the most dangerous moments in my whole life, I wasn't thinking about throwing in the towel. Maybe Don Pacho thought that I was reconsidering my commitment after Sincelejo so I'll let him think that if that's the reason why I will end up being worth almost three quarters of a billion dollars at the end.

"Are you ready to get going with the next set of pick-ups?" Don Pacho asked.

"I am," I responded.

This coming Thursday I would be flying to the Dominican Republic for the first pick-up in the south west end of the country near a city called Barahona; a bay city. Being a shorter trip I was thinking about asking Brooke if she would want to come and have a short two-day vacation in the Caribbean with me. She and Christian David could enjoy the beach while I did the job and I'd be back the same day to enjoy some much needed family time. After dropping them off back at home Saturday morning I would then fly to Uruguay followed by a whole week here at home before taking off on Friday, this time to Portugal. If I hadn't sworn off doing multiple pick-ups in one trip, I would do Portugal, Greece and the Ivory Coast; however, I'm done with that insanity.

The conversation changed from the upcoming trips to a short tutorial on how the next payments would be made via wire transfer. Not being knowledgeable in how to go about it, Don Pacho offered to have his people around the world set me up with several bank accounts for my money. In conclusion, I brought up the imminent dinner with the Director of the DEA here in Miami and told him how he lived down the street from me.

"So Mr. Bruce Haight is your neighbor?" he chuckled. "I'm not surprised that he wants to get close to you."

"That guy has tried to pin stuff on me for quite some time," he complained.

I don't know why I was so surprised at Don Pacho knowing who this guy was already. I'm sure he knows a whole lot more than just who the man is and what his job entails. It wouldn't be farfetched to think that Don Pacho already has that name in his little black pocket book.

Christian David and I made our way back home in time to get this kid in the bath followed by bed time. I couldn't help but think on how this kid was growing so fast and the fact that we could secure his future along with Rocky's in a matter of months. Not only did I want to secure my own family's future but that of all our family members, Brooke's and mine.

What is the point of having all that money if you don't use it for what matters most in life?

That's what this is all about.

Tomorrow was going to be a very busy day. First, I would be going to the office in the morning; my first day in the new building. I'm only working half a day because I had Brooke set up an appointment with the owners of her studio at 1 p.m.; time to put this money to good use. Following that meeting Brooke had asked me if she could introduce me to a couple of dance teachers at her studio; a set of twins that had been looking for an investor to expand their brand of rompers designed for dancers and fitness minded people. Brooke, Christian David and I had a late lunch at the Cheesecake Factory and shortly after, I returned to the office for a few hours. I wanted to begin my search for two teams of programmers; one team would develop an app and the other a website. Since having the start-up capital was never going to be an issue or obstacle ever again, I decided to get moving on these two projects as soon as possible.

"Did he go down easy?" Brooke asked as I tiptoed out of Christian David's room.

"Yeah, he didn't even finish watching the episode of Gummi Bears," I replied.

"When and where will you be traveling again?" Brooke asked as we pulled a couple of stools in the kitchen and decided to finish off a half-eaten watermelon.

"As always you read my thoughts; I was going to bring that up," I answered. "Would you and Christian David like to come with me to the Dominican Republic this Thursday?"

"Thursday to Saturday; I would leave you guys at the resort for only a bit while I got the job done and would be back at night leaving us with all of Friday to have fun," I added.

"That sounds amazing! I will have to get a sub for my Thursday classes but we should be good," she answered with a smile; nothing better than having a happy wife.

"We would be safe to go right?" Brooke asked while scraping the bottom of the hollowed-out watermelon.

"Of course princess, it's not like I'm taking you to the actual excavation site," I chuckled and immediately realized that I may have given her a reason to worry.

"How is the excavation dangerous?" she asked without skipping a heartbeat.

"I meant for the digging and all that," I answered non-convincingly.

"Are you telling me the truth Juan?" She asked with an investigative tone. She can always see right through me.

"That's the only danger to you, right?" she asked. "Unless there's something you're not telling me about your trip to Colombia."

"Hey, don't overthink it too much," I replied. "I am safe and protected at all these sites."

"Protected from what?" she continued.

"Alright princess, I need to use the bathroom," I answered trying to end the spontaneous interrogation.

The last thing I need is for her to know what went down in Colombia and that there is a real danger out there for me. I doubt that we'll run into anything similar in the Dominican Republic though.

TUESDAY NOVEMBER 10TH, 2015 – MIAMI, FL

This morning I woke up full of energy and excitement; I would be playing investor today acquiring one of the most popular, profitable and successful dance studios in all of Greater Miami. But first I made it to the office and got to do a little work in my own office; the office with a billion dollar view. My corner office faces south east with a jaw dropping view of the bay towards Brickell and Virginia Key.

I got my work done extra fast, maybe a little too fast because now I had an hour to spare before the meeting. I decided to get a little head start and do a general Miami search for programmers but it was just too overwhelming. To minimize the hassle I sent a quick email to the Computer Science department over at the University of Miami offering paid internships for 8-10 students interested in my two projects. In the meantime I pulled out my credit card and purchased a couple of domains starting with JogaFutebol.com and iDazzl.com; two soon-to-be billion dollar tech behemoths.

At 1 p.m., Brooke and I enjoyed a successful meeting with the owners, husband and wife, who decided to finally retire by starting with the sale of the studio which consisted of three locations each with very high traffic and following. Their asking price was $4.1 million but we negotiated the price down to $3.7 million with an all cash offer. Brooke was now the proud owner and president of her own very successful dance studio; one of the best feelings in the world for me. After shaking hands we set up a day and time to get the paperwork completed. Brooke then took me to one of the upstairs dance rooms were the twins were finishing up a Hip Hop class.

"Honey, this is Katie and this is Kellie Cockrell," Brooke introduced me.

We had another successful meeting; the twins had started their brand of rompers shortly after completing their undergraduate degrees. They grew their brand organically mainly by word of mouth but had reached a point where an investment was needed for growth. Their brand katieandkellie was used by many of the students throughout the three locations of our studio but most importantly, other dancers across studios in Miami and even in Los Angeles were using katieandkellie rompers. We made a $100K investment for 33% of their company. Now it was time to go and celebrate a huge step in our lives.

The Cheesecake Factory never disappoints; we had an awesome meal as a family leaving us ten pounds heavier at the end. We were able to discuss our upcoming travel plans for Thanksgiving in the next couple of weeks. I would return from the Portugal job on Monday the 23rd and we would take Don Pacho's jet back to Utah the following day; we would be staying at Brooke's parents' house in Draper until Saturday the 28th. I proposed to Brooke that all three of them would fly there on Monday and I would stay in Europe to complete the Greece job. I would then fly into Utah the day before Thanksgiving but she insisted that I stay the whole week with the family. I ended up pushing the Greece job to the 30th of this month going into the first week of December. Lastly, we began looking at dates for the dinner with the Haights and decided to do it on the Friday after returning from Greece; Brooke and I would be going together leaving Christian David with my parents who would be visiting us for a week since my sister-in-law would not be returning to Florida with us.

Wednesday flew by in a blink of an eye. It was a pretty chill day at work; Brooke had a doctor's appointment at noon which I went to followed with a couple of meetings at work. To close the day, Brooke and Christian David accompanied me to my indoor soccer game with my Guatemalan friends. On our way home we stopped to get some Gelato and a few groceries; nothing too exciting but still important family memories nonetheless. After putting the little man to sleep I went over the coordinates for the job in the Dominican Republic while Brooke packed a bag for her and Christian David.

THURSDAY NOVEMBER 12TH, 2015

Don Pacho's driver picked us up at 10 a.m.; Christian David was a little cranky since he didn't sleep well- which I'm blaming on the ice cream from yesterday. The jet took us into the international airport in Santo Domingo; once I made sure that my family was settled in and comfortable in the resort I jumped in an SUV, met the team and began working. The drive from the airport to the excavation site was quite a ways away, according to the GPS it would be a little under three hours to the outskirts of Barahona. Luckily our cargo plane would be waiting for us at a municipal airport nearby. In similar fashion as in previous jobs the excavation was completed in a few hours, actually in less time than the combined time driving there and back to Santo Domingo.

After seeing the next $600 million take off aboard the much smaller Super Hercules, in comparison to our first plane of course, I made the trek back to the resort where Brooke and Christian David had had a fun day at the beach and were getting ready for bed. Despite being tired and dehydrated due to the humid weather I did not want to call it a night and go to bed right away. After all today we were $12 million richer; we needed to celebrate somehow.

FRIDAY NOVEMBER 13TH, 2015 – SANTO DOMINGO, DOMINICAN REPUBLIC

Friday the 13th was spent in its entirety with my wonderful family. We played in the ocean first thing in the morning right before enjoying some awesome Dominican Mangu for breakfast in the Colonial Zone of Santo Domingo. Don Pacho had insisted that we visit Calle el Conde specifically for the best local food according to him on the island. The rest of the day was spent sightseeing and enjoying the beauty of this country; no wonder Christopher Columbus fell in love with this island as soon as he touched dry land. The night ended with a party for adults only and hosted by the JW Marriott where we were staying. They had a fully staffed recreation room for the kids; Christian David had a blast. Brooke and I got to enjoy 1-on-1 time dancing to Fulanito, a Dominican merengue group that I had grown up listening to back in Utah.

Our short business/family trip ended Saturday morning as we flew back to Miami. I chose to ride with my two loves in Don Pacho's Rolls Royce Phantom back home while the jet was prepped for the long flight to Uruguay later today.

"Juan, thank you for taking us with you," Brooke said. "We loved being together as a family."

"Please be safe and return to us soon," she added as she leaned over to kiss me.

"Princess, I wouldn't have it another way," I quickly responded as I kissed her, Christian David and Rocky who was still cooking in the oven; having two kids will be awesome.

We crossed the Caribbean once again on our way to South America and made it to Montevideo just before midnight. The excavation in the morning would take place in a small town called Minas; a two hour drive north east of the capital. I actually had an uncle-by-marriage that was originally from there. Upon arriving to Carrasco international airport I was met by a man driving a Maserati who introduced himself as simply Diego.

Diego took me to the Belmont House hotel where I would spend the night until it was time to get moving again. The short 15 minute drive took double the time due to unusual heavy traffic at that time.

"Is traffic always this bad?" I asked Diego while yawning.

"It is, Avenida Italia is always like this when Uruguay plays," he explained. "La Celeste beat Colombia tonight at the Centenario in route for qualifying for the next World Cup."

The bumper to bumper traffic was covered with dozens of Uruguayan flags waving and never ending car horns. I miss the passion for this sport that the US is lacking tenfold.

"I will be here to pick you up in the morning at 10 a.m. if that's alright with you." He asked as he pulled up to the front of the hotel and stopped behind a bus.

"You're a wise man Diego!" I replied with a smile. "No need to get little sleep."

"I will see you tomorrow," I added as a bell boy took out my single bag out of the trunk.

"Welcome to the Belmont House Sir," the young bell boy said as he had me follow him to the double rotating doors.

I glanced at the group exiting the bus and immediately recognized a couple of faces; it was James Rodriguez, David Ospina and the rest of the Colombian national team that were staying here too. Talk about lucky timing. I was able to get a couple of pictures with some of the players before checking in at the front desk. Once in my suite, I didn't BS around at all and I just crashed. I sent a good night's message to Brooke and turned off the lights.

SUNDAY NOVEMBER 15TH, 2015 – MONTEVIDEO, URUGUAY

Woke up in a great and cheery mood; enhanced by the wonderful five-Star breakfast in my room before heading out in a heavily guarded caravan. I was protected more heavily than the bus carrying a whole soccer squad representing a nation; the power of money at its finest. Then again I should be referred as the $36 billion man so the protection is part of the job description.

This time around our caravan decided to go with the 'Italian Mafia' feel. We were nine vehicles consisting of the white Maserati I was in, two black Mercedes Benz sedans, an 18 wheeler, and three police patrol cars including two police officers on motorcycles. Not too inconspicuous in my opinion.

The Minas job moved forward without any delay and we were back in the airport ahead of schedule. The Hercules was loaded and ready in line for take-off. Before I could start counting my next $12 million I began hearing sirens and immediately saw a group of white SUVs driving towards our plane blocking the take-off. As we drove up to the plane we noticed that they were all INTERPOL vehicles. This is the last thing I need right now.

"Let me do the talking," Diego said, "The Uruguayan office of the INTERPOL is a joke."

"Be my guest Diego," I replied.

Diego approached the group of men that appeared to be in charge and were calling all the shots. After a few minutes of chatting with them he placed a call and handed the phone to one of the men. In a matter of minutes the plane was given the green light to proceed with take-off.

Diego informed me that someone had made an anonymous call to the Uruguayan INTERPOL office claiming that the plane was carrying several tons of cocaine heading to the United States.

"Who was on the phone?" I asked as I saw our plane fly into the horizon.

"The President of Uruguay," he answered while I waited for him to crack a laugh or see a smile. "Well, someone in the President's office."

He was serious, we even had the President of Uruguay and his cabinet bought off. Don Pacho's reach and influence is far beyond what it was in the 80's and 90's. While the Colombian and United States government opened champagne bottles celebrating the "defeat" of Pablo Escobar and the Medellin Cartel, the reality was that the cartel had only morphed into the global organization that he has operated for the last two decades.

If it's any indication of his reach, the most current list of pick-up locations for me is truly overwhelming. So far I've completed all 5 Colombian jobs; the Dominican Republic and Uruguay gigs are also complete with Portugal, Greece and the Ivory Coast up next. But the list only grows to (in alphabetical order):

Algeria - Argentina - Aruba - Australia - Bangladesh - Belarus - Benin - Bolivia - British Virgin Islands - Burkina Faso - Cambodia - Canada - Costa Rica - Cuba - Curacao - Cyprus - Czech Republic - Denmark - Dominica - Estonia - Fiji - France - Gabon - Ghana - Guadeloupe - Haiti - Hungary - Italy - Iceland – Ireland - Japan - Latvia - Lithuania - Malawi - Martinique - Moldova - Mongolia - Morocco - Myanmar - New Zealand - Philippines - Poland - Romania - Serbia - Slovakia - Sweden - Switzerland - Thailand – Venezuela – Vietnam.

MONDAY NOVEMBER 16TH, 2015 – MIAMI, FL

Back in Miami, Brooke and Christian David were at the airport to pick me up; wonderful surprise. While we had our chef prepare a succulent lunch for us in our kitchen, I jumped online for a few minutes to confirm that both transfers had been made to my accounts. There in front of me were two transfers of $12 million each; our net worth rising to over 50 million dollars since the dance studio deal hasn't gone through yet.

After the post-lunch splash fight in our pool I made a call to my dad to discuss a couple of things including some business topics. Now that the start-up capital was abounding, the next group of investments would be in association with my dad. First on the list was opening five franchises from brands like Subway and Dollar Tree; this was my dad's early birthday present since it had been part of his plans for many years. My mom also jumped on the investment train by suggesting that we invested in a couple of her acquaintances that needed capital to expand. The first one was a clinic that helped people with no health insurance and high deductibles called HOPE Family Medical Center. I could see that this would be a great investment especially on the moral arena; my introduction to philanthropy. The second one was a friend of my mom's that owned a Merle Norman Cosmetics franchise but needed a small investment to add a boutique and medical spa/studio to her current Draper location. In conclusion, I reminded my dad of a restaurant idea that I had had since I was a teenager.

As a Colombian, oddly enough, my favorite food was not Colombian but Mexican and I had always wanted to one day own a Mexican restaurant. I would name it Malagueña after the song, and it would be a combination of a botanical garden and a high-end but affordable restaurant; a place where you could be serenated by a mariachi band while enjoying a wonderful meal in a serene, lush and uplifting environment.

"Juan Camilo, you don't know anything about running a restaurant," my dad warned.

"True, but remember when I was 21 and I was a loan officer before the recession?" I asked. "One of the few deals I closed was for that friend of yours that had a Mexican restaurant for over 20 years."

"He had to close the restaurant a few years ago," he replied.

"I know, but that means that he'll be eager and available to work with us in getting Malagueña up and ready," I added.

The next couple of months flew by at an astonishing speed. I completed the Portugal job prior to spending Thanksgiving with both sets of families. Upon returning to Florida with my parents, Brooke and I spent five days in Greece; amazing time spent with my beautiful wife and collected an additional $12 million pay check. We met up with the Haights for that dinner where I finally met the DEA guy; our wives have become pretty good friends since then, unfortunately. After Greece things got pretty heavy and busy starting with the Ivory Coast job followed by the long laundry-list of pick-ups. I racked up the sky miles traveling to what felt like, every corner of the world.

Brooke's pregnancy kept progressing quite nicely, Christian David went through a crazy growth spurt, and the bank accounts kept growing steadily into the hundreds of millions while learning the ins and outs of this emerging global organization.

During the Christmas season, I had the opportunity to spoil Brooke, Christian David, my parents, Brooke's parents and even my whole family in Colombia like I never could've imagined before. I bought homes, cars, paid college tuitions, paid off debts, started businesses and even created jobs for many of them.

The only reason I've been involved in all of this from the beginning has been only for the welfare of my entire family; it's an indescribable feeling being able to lend a helping hand to everyone.

SATURDAY MARCH 12TH, 2016

March 18, aka Rocky's big day, is in less than a week. I only have one last pick-up to complete before we welcome our baby boy and collect the last $12 million bringing my total earnings to a modest $690 million fortune. In other news, Don Pacho insisted in coming along to the last site in Mongolia. We fly out later today and with the 12-hour difference we should be back no later than Tuesday or possibly Wednesday. After five months of traveling to every continent, digging up $36 billion and coming close to death on a couple of occasions, I have come to the end of the road; time for me to make a decision. I think it's time to go into retirement from this glamorous industry, focus on my well-paying corporate job and family business empire.

Before heading out to the airport I was able to be present at Brooke's third to last check-up before Rocky makes his first public appearance. The delivery date is still looking good for next Friday; Christian David kept his initial delivery date so I hope Rocky cooperates as well.

After the doctor's visit we swung by the airport to pick up Brooke's mom who would be staying with us for the next month or so. I said my goodbyes to Brooke and Christian David before the little man's bath time.

We began our 21+ hour red eye flight towards Ulaanbaatar, Mongolia, just after 8 p.m. - Saturday - Miami time. We touched down in the Mongolian capital Monday morning at 6:30 a.m.; we skipped a whole day flying, talk about messing with your mind and body. The temperature was a toasty 21 degrees with lows tonight in the single digits; just our luck, the coldest day for the next two weeks. I dropped the ball for this trip by not checking the weather before making out here. Don Pacho had one of our men get us some Nomadic clothing from a street vendor. We looked like natives with our nomad deels and hats.

The GPS pinpointed the site just over three hours away directly south from Ulaanbaatar. However, since the set-up for this last pick-up was a little different from the rest, we wouldn't be able to get there by land but only by air. Our caravan this time around would consist of two old Soviet Yak-24 helicopters for transporting the expensive cargo. As we made our way to the site we had to give the coordinates over the radio to the men guiding the laborers who apparently were all on horseback coming from a neighboring village. The coordinates showed that we would be digging for the last 50 drums at the foot of the Khangai and Altai Mountains near the Gobi Desert.

Upon arriving I glanced out the window to see more than 50 horsemen; nomads in all sense of the word. Once the excavation was underway I couldn't help but think how the current setting looked like a scene out of an Indiana Jones movie; we had truly traveled back in time.

"Juancho, one of the reasons I wanted to be here was to walk where Genghis Khan walked," Don Pacho said. "The man was one of the most powerful men to ever live."

"Since a young age I've always been fascinated by Mongolian empires like the Xiongnu, Xianbei, Rouran, the Turkic Khaganate but especially the Mongol Empire spearheaded by Genghis Khan himself," he added.

"The little I know about him is that he was a ruthless and barbaric tyrant," I replied as we watched the first helicopter being loaded.

"I respect Genghis Khan not only for all he accomplished in regards to conquering so much of the world," he explained, "but the loyalty he commanded from all people, whether they were part of his empire or not."

Based on history it's obvious that Escobar emulated a lot of his behavior on Genghis Khan's ruthlessness and intimidation; the Medellin cartel was his Mongol Empire and now it's the whole world.

After loading up the second helicopter we made our way back to the airport where the Hercules was already there. As we witnessed the last cargo take-off from "The Land of the Eternal Blue Sky" as Mongolia is known for, I wasn't surprised to have mixed feelings. On one hand I was filthy rich and practically 'out' of the game, but on the other I was curious to see where I could take this to. After all, Don Pacho had promised to make me the 2nd richest man in the world.

Despite being exhausted Don Pacho insisted that we go have dinner in Dubai since it was on our way home. I explained to him that I needed to get back as soon as possible so if we did then we would have to floor it in case Brooke went into labor early.

"Juancho, we need to celebrate the tremendous success we had with all of the jobs," Don Pacho couldn't hide his excitement as we took off in his jet. "It's not every day that your net worth increases in the billions of dollars."

Once in Dubai we were greeted by a friend of Don Pacho's, owner of the restaurant where we would be dining later. Before we got in the elevator he had us make a quick stop at a boutique in the ground level of the Burj Al Arab hotel. There was a required dress code at the Al Muntaha restaurant; the first seven-star restaurant that I've ever heard of.

With the Arabian sunset as a back drop and the stunning 360 degree view of Dubai, the staff proceeded to royally pamper us with a large selection of world-renowned appetizers. The environment was truly electric with a hint of power, it was palpable. I felt like a Sultan. My family's economic future was set; I felt I had to toast to our accomplishment.

"Don Pacho, I'd like to offer a toast," I began, "for the wonde…"

"Juancho, stop!" he interrupted me as he signaled our waiter to our table.

"I understand your decision to not drink, but if we're doing this toast I need you to accompany me with an appropriate drink," he added.

I have never given in to peer-pressure but under the circumstances I decided to just try it this once. We were quickly brought some champagne to continue our celebration; I initially thought a glass would suffice but after a few I began feeling a buzz and decided to stop.

"Juancho, I have waited many years for this moment," Don Pacho explained, "and thanks to you my friend I have become the richest man in the world."

"I want you to know that I have never trusted anyone as much as I do you Juancho," he began slurring his words as the champagne continued to flow for the next couple of hours.

After enjoying our meal Don Pacho had me follow him to the balcony overseeing the bay and asked me to join him in one last toast.

"Here is to working together for the unforeseeable future - in the good times and in the bad," he shouted over the outdoor music while holding on to the railing since he was overly tipsy.

"We should give ourselves a name Juancho; a team name, worthy of a powerful duo," he added as he gave me a hug and a kiss on the cheek.

"How about 'The Extraditables'?" I mumbled the first thing that came to mind not thinking clearly due to the booze.

Almost immediately his countenance changed, it seemed that the effects of the night's alcohol had also escaped him; he sobered up instantly. I suddenly couldn't hear any music or any of the people talking around us. He stared into my eyes and I knew right then that I had just given away what I had promised myself over and over to never reveal, especially to him. I had just confessed to Pablo Escobar that I knew who he was; as if my life needed any more danger in it.

My first thought turned to Brooke, Christian David and Rocky. What should I do? Where to run away to? Who to go to? In a matter of seconds I went through multiple possible scenarios and outcomes; I was truly screwed. I did not know what to expect.

The drive back to the jet was in complete silence as well as the first couple of hours in the air. Any desire to sleep quickly left me. It seemed appropriate to be awake and alert as much as possible under the current circumstances. How do you get a conversation started with the world's most powerful and ruthless criminal after you've blown his cover and he knows it?

I felt the need to send Brooke a message telling her how much I loved her and the boys. I was about to hit send when a hand swung past me and took the phone out of my hands.

"Juancho, who are we writing to this late?" asked Don Pacho as he turned an overhead light to read what the message said.

"Don Pacho, I was writing Brooke," I explained somewhat nervously. "I'm sorry, did I wake you up?"

"Juancho, I think we need to have a little chat before we make it back to Miami," he explained as he pressed send and handed the phone back to me.

"Sure Don Pacho, about what?" I asked trying to downplay the strong feeling of hostility that quickly filled the cabin.

"I think we know the 'what'," he replied as he pulled out his little black pocket book and placed it on his lap.

"You've been working for me for some time now Juan," he said, "Have you enjoyed the time working for me?"

"I have Don Pacho, without a doubt," I answered.

"I want to believe that I've treated you and your family as if you were my own family, am I right to think so?" he continued.

"Yes sir," I replied. "Brooke and I are truly grateful for everything that you've done for us."

"That's good to hear," he added.

"Remember our little conversation about Genghis Khan back in Mongolia?" he asked.

"I do," I answered as I began feeling sweat rolling down my back.

"Another reason why I admire Genghis Khan on top of the many other reasons," he explained, "is spot on with what you said about him back at the excavation site."

"Do you remember what you said?" he asked trying to make me repeat it.

"I don't I'm sorry," I replied knowing well what I had said.

"A crucial trait that he had and executed very well through the years was," he explained, "the easiness to be barbaric and a tyrant throughout his reign."

"You see, he couldn't have achieved all he did had he not be willing to do what was necessary to accomplish his goals as a leader of his army and his people," he added.

"Juancho, I am a natural born leader," he continued, "and I have the same trait, it has never been an issue for me."

"I don't let anything or anyone stand in the way between me and all of my goals," he emphasized. "That is why my empire exceeds the $100 billion mark today.

"Having said that I always make it a priority to care about the people working for me; it's very important to me to take care of them and their loved ones," he said as he opened one of the pages from his little black pocket book.

It took me a moment to realize that the names he began reading out loud to me were my own family members. He listed personal things from each member living here in the US and in Colombia; things that not even all family members knew about each other. He mentioned a cousin of mine back in Colombia that had diabetes and the results of her last doctor's visit, he mentioned the costs of speech therapy that one of Brooke's cousin's kids had each month. He even mentioned the exact amount owed by my aunt and her husband for my late Grandmother's house. I realized the purpose behind listing all these things; he was making it clear to me that he had eyes and ears on all of my family. He was making it known to me that he was in control of their safety.

"Juancho, as I've said before," he reminded me, "family – in this case, Brooke and your two boys are the most important people in your life and my advice is, hold them close and take care of them."

"The worst thing in the world would be if you lost them due to making a bad decision," he added.

The SOB was threatening my family right to my face.

TUESDAY MARCH 15TH, 2016

As we touched down in Miami, I had to ask my driver to turn around and head for the hospital since my mother-in-law had just texted me that Brooke was finally in labor. All I could think of was the safety of my wife and kids. I was in a complex situation where I could not turn to anyone. Not only would no one believe me, but most importantly, Don Pacho had eyes and ears everywhere as he made it known to me. I was truly alone in all of this.

I ran into my boy and his Grandma in the reception area on my way in. A member of the hospital staff took me straight to Brooke who was in a pre-delivery room; an expectant mother alone with her contractions. I am so grateful for her, not only is she the toughest woman I know but also the best wife and mother we could ever have. I don't think I can get myself to tell Brooke of the situation especially right now. The last thing we need is to turn a joyous moment in our lives into a complete spin and get lost in a sea of uncertainty and worry for the future.

After a long seven hours my Brooke gave birth to our beautiful baby boy, Rocky Alexander Arias, weighing a healthy 8 pounds 5 ounces and measuring a good 22 inches. He was here, the 4th member of our small family; holding him made every worry in the world leave my mind for a moment. I had put my family into a dangerous situation and I needed to find a way to resolve this.

The last day at the hospital we got to Skype with some of the family back in Utah to introduce the little man. After the video I received a call from my dad asking me if everything was ok; he said he could tell I had something on my mind during the video chat; he could sense I seemed distracted. All I could come up with was some bogus story about back in the office.

"Juan Camilo, leave work at work and enjoy this moment with Brooke," he advised. "Nothing in this world can measure up to the happiness that comes from within the walls of your own home."

"Money and power will only distract you from what's really important," he added.

Wise advice from my dad but my distractions at this moment came in fear and anger - fear for the welfare of my wife, kids and family members here and in Colombia – anger because of a human being's natural instinct to protect their own.

A few days ago I was checking out my Facebook feed and watched a shared video of a mother rat fighting a snake that had her young by the neck and was dragging it into the long grass; an imminent and cruel death. After a fight that lasted a good minute and a half the snake finally let go and slid away. The mother did not stop; it also jumped into the long grass and went after the snake until it was sure that the danger was no longer there. The smaller and more insignificant pray overcame the bigger and intimidating predator by sheer fear and anger.

Once we were home I made sure that Brooke and Rocky were settled in, now it was time to get some Father-Son time with Christian David; the little man needed some attention so we headed to the movies to watch Zootopia. After a little ice cream and playground time we headed back home to get this little man in the bath.

I was about to rinse the shampoo off when a call came in; Don Pacho and his perfect timing as always.

"Juancho, congratulations on the baby!" exclaimed Don Pacho, "How is Brooke doing?"

He was back to his cheerful self, as if the conversation where he put a price on my family's safety never happened; just swept the threat under the rug.

"I need you to come with me to Las Vegas this weekend," he ordered, "We have some important business to attend to."

After hanging up I continued with Christian David's bath and asked him to tilt his head back to rinse off the shampoo. It was right then that a thought, a solution to our problem, flew in out of nowhere.

I needed to take advantage of the fear and anger, in other words, I needed to be like the mother rat and face the predator. Only then would I be able to keep my family safe.

The solution to the problem is clear.

I need to kill him.

The next step would be to come up with a detailed plan; the where, the when and the how. A man that has faced death on several occasions in the past definitely knows a thing or two about survival and sleeping with one eye open at night. That is why I'm the only that can get this done – he trusts me.

I dedicated the remainder of the week to Brooke by taking a mini-week vacation from work so I could help out around the house with cleaning and the boys. My mother-in-law is a huge help but extra hands never hurt anyone. Brooke can now focus entirely on a full recovery.

FRIDAY MARCH 18TH, 2016 – LAS VEGAS, NV

On Friday we left for Las Vegas in the early afternoon, upon arriving we were checked in at the Bellagio's Chairman Suite or as the staff called it, 'The Don Pacho Suite.' I was told that during the latest remodel of this suite, the hotel made sure to ask Don Pacho for his input. The business that we were attending to would take place in a couple of hours over at The Palms where Don Pacho's associates were staying at.

"Juancho, I'm feeling lucky," said Don Pacho, "Let's go downstairs for a little bit and get the juices going."

As usual, several attractive gold diggers made their way over to us as Don Pacho played a few hands of poker; lost and gained a few million just pocket change for him. We made our way over to the Hugh Hefner Sky Villa at The Palms where a good dozen men had been living it up like rock stars for a while now. As soon as Don Pacho and I walked in the atmosphere changed dramatically from party to business – a few dozen women were asked to head to the pool area as we conducted business.

The men at this meeting were the major players overseeing the "Golden Triangle" in South East Asia. Don Pacho introduced me to the main man, a business associate of his for many years now, Mr. Sa. He was the nephew of renowned Burmese drug warlord Khun Sa. The man had taken over the empire shortly after his billionaire uncle passed away in 2007; around the time when Don Pacho and Mr. Sa were introduced to each other.

These individuals were among the most powerful men in the world managing millions of tons of opium and heroin base originating in

Myanmar and distributed by maritime transport compliments of Don Pacho & Co.

Mr. Sa also oversaw the multi-billion dollar Chinese production of precursor chemicals necessary for the production of cocaine, heroin, ecstasy and crystal meth on a global scale. I was never a fan of Chemistry in school but some of the few recognizable ones were Acetic Anhydride, Ephedrine and Pseudoephedrine.

In addition to his transportation services and distribution expertise, Don Pacho is also a partner with Mr. Sa, which shouldn't surprise anyone since his reach is never-ending, he truly has his hand in everything. Don Pacho has more reach and influence than some presidents do in their own countries. During the meeting he had a few of his men present the current needs for their respective coastal ports, ports in areas like Guangdong, Tianjin, Shanghai and Qingdao who were continually expanding despite the many unsuccessful attempts from the authorities to stop them.

One of the main topics of the night was about the necessary push for expansion in the Indian market; this group only managed to infiltrate 22% of the market and fell short to the 'Golden Crescent'. Afghanistan is the player that all of these men want to dethrone.

To close the meeting the last topic addressed was sort of a To-Do list for improving the logistics on distribution from and to locations like: Burma, Cambodia, Hong Kong, Taiwan, Thailand and the United States. In regards to the US, the priority was to add more transit routes using the Canadian border.

"Juancho, next weekend you and I are flying out to Vancouver to meet with some of our Canadian friends to discuss the subject," Don Pacho leaned and whispered in my ear.

Once the change from business to party mode had been made I decided to walk the strip by myself. For one I needed fresh air, well at least air – Las Vegas has no fresh air, and second, I wanted to get Christian David something at the M&M store. Despite being 3 a.m., I didn't feel tired enough to hit the sack right away so after walking most of the strip I made my way in to The Venetian; I just needed some gelato and a bench to take some time off and just think. While looking at the gondoliers pass by below me I came to a realization; in the last months I had transitioned from a trustworthy employee or courier for Don Pacho to an important and powerful drug dealer that other important and powerful men respected.

The same recurring thought kept coming to me about the time Brooke told me that she had not married a drug trafficker and emphasized that our marriage depended on it; talk about standing in between a rock and a hard place. How would she ever understand that I'm a drug trafficker by obligation? Here I am with a net worth of $690 million wishing I could give it all back just so things could be back to normal. No drug dealing. No impending danger to my family; just Brooke, my boys and an ordinary life.

Back in my room I went straight to bed despite my brain being completely awake. I kept searching for a believable way to kill him. The options are slim when the person you're trying to get rid of is more powerful than a president. How do you plan out a hit that only you are capable of performing?

I pulled out my phone for a while to change things a bit and distract me for a while. I noticed my Facebook account was full of comments to a post that I had been tagged to. My junior high chemistry teacher had passed away a few days ago after a long struggle with cancer and all the comments were from former students, many of them classmates of mine. Mrs. Shapiro's 7th grade class at good ol' Eisenhower Jr. High was one of those classes that I simply wanted to forget as I got older. It seemed like all students loved her without end, however I was definitely not one of the best students in that subject and my grades showed that. I was reading some of the tagged names on the post when I came across a name that I had not heard in more than 15 years, Neal Finnick. Neal had had his fair share of encounters with bullies being the smart kid and the bullying always seemed to happen at a time when I was nearby; I was never bullied or was a bully myself so naturally I was inclined to help him. Neal was the only reason why I didn't fail chemistry completely and was able to scrape through. The last time I heard of him was in 9th grade when his dad made the news after receiving a nobel prize for something chemistry related; they moved somewhere back east before the end of the school year.

I clicked on his name to open his profile and see what he was up to nowadays. I wasn't completely surprised when I read that he was a big shot chemist at MIT; a successful published chemist. Not only that but the profile pictures I saw of Neal it seemed that he had spent some time in the gym in addition to the lab. Based on the messages it seemed that almost everyone was planning on being present at the funeral the day after tomorrow; Neal was one of them.

What if I used chemistry to resolve my current problem? Neal could be the answer.

SATURDAY MARCH 19TH, 2016

After finally falling asleep and waking up at almost noon I decided to tell Don Pacho that I wouldn't be flying back to Miami with him. Instead, I was planning on flying up to Utah to attend the funeral. I was beginning to grow paranoid that Don Pacho not only was tapping my phone and having my loved ones and me followed, but also was keeping track of my actions on the web. Luckily I had a believable story for me going my own separate way.

"Juancho, good luck on your trip," said Don Pacho with a smirk, "I'll keep an eye on Brooke and your boys."

I could feel my blood starting to boil. I need to take care of him as soon as possible.

Once we went our separate ways I took a minute to call Brooke and check up on her and the boys. In turn I told her about my plans to spend a couple of days in Utah.

"Tell Christian David that if he's a good boy for mommy, I'll bring him a present," I said as the girl behind the desk looked into flights heading to Utah.

"I'm sorry Sir, there are no flights going out of McCarran today," she advised. "There is one through another airline taking off at 8 a.m. tomorrow."

Ugh, I'm done with Vegas; I need to get out of here. I decided to just drive but the bad news kept coming. Due to the time of the year every car rental company was out of cars. No way in hell was I going to spend another night in Vegas away from my family.

As I was about to step out of the last car rental company I was stopped by the manager; he told me that the system showed one available car at one of their locations about 20 miles from here. After much frustration and an Uber ride I was finally on my way to Utah in a small Ford Focus. I forgot how crappy these cars were; I took driver's Ed with these things during the summer before my junior year of high school. On the flipside I was on my way out of this place.

After passing St. George I decided to call my parents to tell them that I was on my way there and should be getting there in about five or five and a half hours all depending on the power of this ruthless speed machine. With the long drive ahead it was time to come up with a sales pitch for Neal.

Hey Neal, so how could I use chemistry to kill someone without leaving evidence or any kind of trace leading back to me? Not quite the desired approach or subtlety.

I drove into the Salt Lake Valley a little past 8 p.m.. I had to call my parents for the address since they had recently moved into the new house I bought for them in Daybreak. Despite just being two in the house, I thought that it would be more than appropriate to buy them a slightly bigger house so that Brooke and I could stay there with the kids when we visited. Part of the reason why I bought that particular house was because we had taken Christian David to a community park with a man-made beach there and he loved it so much that the only option was to buy a lakeside home.

Despite the chilly Utah March weather, we spent Sunday afternoon in the backyard which has easy access to a mini private beach area. If it wasn't for the current state of affairs that I currently find myself in it could've been a very relaxed evening alongside my parents. Just like before, my dad and I had a conversation that arose from a similar comment he made when we were still in the hospital with Rocky. I thought I could hide my worry from them by putting a happy façade but I can't fool the two people that raised me. To avoid giving away the truth I opted for a weak promise to tell them when the time was right; if that time ever comes is a topic of discussion for another day.

MONDAY MARCH 21ST, 2016 – SALT LAKE CITY, UT

The funeral took place in a cemetery a couple of blocks down the street from our old junior high. After the burial Mrs. Shapiro's family members announced that they had asked for permission to use the school for a small get-together/lunch to celebrate Mrs. Shapiro's life and love of teaching. This being my second funeral ever attended I felt a little guilty that the main motive for me being there was not Mrs. Shapiro. After being approached by several unrecognizable people from back in the day and talking about what I was doing nowadays, I finally had the opportunity to approach Neal. Neal had by far the biggest transformation of everyone in attendance. His success was definitely expected with how smart and devoted he was to his studies, but the transformation I was referring to was purely on the physical; not to mention the girl he was with, never would've pictured old Neal with a future girlfriend or spouse like that.

I was surprised how excited Neal was to see me; he recognized me immediately and had a smile from ear to ear. We spoke for a good amount of time about the same things, what we were doing nowadays and so forth; for obvious reasons I had to edit several things in my life or current resume.

Just as human nature goes, everyone was quietly measuring each other's success by how they were dressed, how they looked after all these years and the coup de gras, what they currently drove. Despite driving in a POS Ford Focus I had no doubt that I had the heaviest pockets in this place but definitely not the cleanest or most honorable money.

It was clear to me that this wasn't the best place or time to discuss what I needed to accomplish with Neal, so I quickly came up with a Plan B. I told him that I had picked up a new hobby over the years in script-writing. I was currently writing a script for a movie where the main character at one point would have to kill the antagonist but the only way to do so was by using his head and expertise in chemistry. From his reaction he seemed

that this would be something he would be willing to help me out with; it

seemed like a fool proof plan so far.

We exchanged numbers and scheduled a lunch meeting in Boston in two

weeks from today. I had always wanted to visit Boston and luckily Don

Pacho had a carwash in the area; I could easily come up with a reason to

fly up there.

TUESDAY MARCH 22ND, 2016 – MIAMI, FL

Back in Miami I had the opportunity to get Christian David ready for

school in the morning and take him myself before going into the office.

The heavy traveling and arrival of Rocky had prevented me from taking

this little guy to school; I still hadn't met his teacher. At school Christian

David was more than excited to show me his school, his classroom, the

toy section and even his hook for his backpack. I was also able to chat a

little with one of his teachers; he had three that handled a good dozen

kids between themselves. Christian David had been improving in his speech really well; I'm so proud of the little guy, I love hearing him communicate well with others.

"We love Christian, he's wonderful!" said another teacher from across the room, "We also loved his Grandpa."

"Excuse me, his Grandpa?" I asked confused.

"Yeah, he came in a few months ago and was absolutely wonderful," she explained, "He brought treats for everyone."

"Tell Don Pacho that we miss him," she added.

After I kissed my boy goodbye and forced a smile as I thanked the ladies for all they do, all I could think about as I walked out of the school was the determination I felt to carry out my plan. If my family had any chance of a safe future it would only be possible with him out of the picture. Boston couldn't come any sooner.

Once in the office I was told by my secretary of a couple of meetings that I had scheduled for today to discuss some marketing needs for several of Don Pacho's corporations. While I turned on my computer I glanced at the TV in search of the morning news; all media outlets were covering a terrorist attack this morning in Brussels, Belgium. Society is going insane, not only the recent terrorist attacks in France and Belgium but now it seems that public shootings are a regular thing now every week.

Two of the corporations that are on the list for discussion today happen to be headquartered in Belgium. One of them is based in Ghent to the north east of the capital exporting machinery and equipment while the other one is in the food service industry providing the food for the European Union and NATO office headquarters in Brussels. Don Pacho told me once that we have a few insiders in both the EU and NATO offices working for us; it would be unusual if we didn't.

The rest of the day went ahead as scheduled, in between meetings I decided to have lunch in my office and do some random shopping online right after I checked my multiple bank accounts with three-quarters of a billion dollars; I check them several times a day, I love seeing it with my own eyes. My mother's birthday was coming up on April 7th and knowing that my parents never really had a honeymoon I went ahead and booked a two-week chartered vacation to Greece; they more than deserve it. My next few purchases were mostly out of impulse; six new soccer jerseys, six new Sottomarino watches, a new white custom ordered Mercedes Benz S63, a $15K diamond Breitling watch, a pair of $200K diamond earrings for Brooke and some cool toys for the boys. It was an expensive day at the office.

At home, our cook had prepared a Mediterranean dinner with some French pastries for dessert. As usual it was a struggle to get Christian David to eat but now with two boys it was entirely up to me to get this guy fed, bathed and put to bed; my mother-in-law went back to Utah this afternoon. During dinner I could tell something was bothering Brooke. I know tired Brooke, exhausted Brooke, even pissed off Brooke; I had never seen this Brooke. Once both boys went down for the night I contemplated on going to play some Futsal at a nearby church where I had started going on the Tuesday nights that I was here; however, I couldn't leave without talking it out with Brooke.

"Princess, are you ok?" I asked in an inquisitive tone as I took off my shoes. "You seem a little off since dinner."

"Juan, when you and I talked about helping your boss with these pick-ups you clearly said, even promised that you would be done after the 60 trips," Brooke said.

"You're still in aren't you?" she asked.

"You lied to me!" she shouted without letting me answer.

"Why do you say I lied?" I asked knowing well I did.

"That trip to Las Vegas and your next trip to Canada," she said on the verge of crying, "you don't want out."

"Do you remember what I told you before you started flying everywhere?" she asked.

"Yes, I do," I responded.

"What did I say Juan?" she raised her voice.

"You said that you didn't marry a drug trafficker," I replied, "and that our marriage depended on it."

"I know that you haven't been completely honest about what you did during those trips," she said.

"If you want a chance of staying married you will tell me everything right now!" she added.

Our conversation went well into the night as I started out with the condo fire, the DEA agents spying on us, followed by the second run-in when I was pulled over and searched for narcotics supposedly. In regards to Colombia, I told her every detail about each pick-up beginning with Medellin and ending with the war zone near Sincelejo. Next, I told her about the Germany/Spain trip prior to the 60 trips that included the meetings, the attendees and who could forget all the run-ins with the girls. I decided to end with the meeting in Las Vegas leaving out completely the most important bit about how I was under the employment of Pablo Escobar; I didn't see the need to include that particular part since it was a very sensitive issue at this present time. I needed to take care of that part before really getting out of the game for good without anything coming back to us.

"Juan, the way I see it is that if you want us to stay together," she said as she wiped her tears, "you will walk up to your boss tomorrow and tell him that you're out."

"What are you going to do?" she asked.

It was already 3 a.m. and all this stress was definitely not healthy for a recovering Brooke. I promised that I would talk with Don Pacho and 'quit' my extracurricular activities with him as his second in command.

"And...?" she added.

"And....what?" I asked.

"You will do it tomorrow," she emphasized.

"Yes, I will do it tomorrow," I replied.

I must have been pretty convincing because she fell asleep in a matter of minutes. I, on the other hand, did not have any desire to sleep. Rocky woke up an hour later so I warmed up some bottled breast milk and changed his diaper so Brooke could get her sleep. Once Rocky was asleep I went back to our room but rather than lying next to Brooke, I sat in our little sitting area next to our master bedroom fireplace. It was obvious that I couldn't comply with Brooke's request but instead I needed to remain close and loyal to Don Pacho so I could carry out my plan.

I needed to prep myself for the next phase of my life; the stress levels were going to peak like never before in my almost 31 years of life. I would basically be living a lie both at home and at work; I needed to keep Brooke and Don Pacho happy as I played a role as the perfect family man and the loyal right-hand man. It won't be easy but it's a necessary evil for the good of my family. They are all that matter.

The rest of the week seemed to drag especially since Brooke was giving me the silent treatment. The morning after our serious conversation she asked me if I had followed through with my promise; I told her that I did but deep down inside she must know that I wasn't going to.

FRIDAY MARCH 25TH, 2016 – VANCOUVER, BC, CANADA

Friday's flight to Vancouver finally came; we took off at noon in the middle of a good Miami down pour. My alibi to Brooke would be that this trip was a weekend corporate getaway with managers for all Slippery Pete's carwashes in Canada; based on the look she gave me I don't think she bought it but still didn't fight me on it. During the lengthy flight Don Pacho decided to go for one of the recliners rather than his bed; he was out after a couple of hours. I couldn't help but think how easy and maybe convenient it would be to kill him here and now. However, I would also have to take care of the pilots and stewardess; I'm not interested in going on a murderous rampage; not yet any way.

After touching down we were taken by Don Pacho's Canadian driver to the biggest mansion I had seen yet; it actually made the local news when he purchased it at $51 million – breaking a record and making it one of the most expensive homes in the Vancouver area. As we pulled in past the gates there were already a dozen cars parked in the rather small driveway. Inside the palace we walked through a perfectly manicured courtyard into a large study with a magnificent view of the English Bay and West Vancouver. There were a couple of dozen men already sitting down waiting for us.

"Gentlemen, thank you for taking time out of your busy schedules to meet us here," Don Pacho said as he wheeled out an old white board.

"We'll be discussing two extremely important topics this evening," Don Pacho said as he took the cap off a marker and began writing. "The first one is in regards to transportation and distribution using this wonderful country."

"The second will be to address and resolve an issue according to our associates in Asia," he added. "It appears that some hiccups have surfaced in our processes and operations that need immediate clarification."

Being the avid and ever knowledgeable strategist, Don Pacho wrote a list of current and new cities that would be vital to our operations. According to him, Canada was not only important because of the Canada/Australia or Canada/Europe connection, but because the Canada/US border had not been utilized or maximized in the most effective way.

"If you believe that your distribution channels and cash flow potential have a cap, then you're going about this the wrong way and simply not being creative enough," Don Pacho warned.

"The usage of both large cities and small cities is key," he added as he pointed at some of the cities on the board.

Vancouver – Lethbridge – Estevan - Winnipeg/Altona - Thunder Bay - Sault Ste Marie – Toronto – Ottawa - Montreal - Saint John.

As Don Pacho wrapped up he walked over to a wood chest and pulled out a bottle.

"Now it's time to discuss our second and final topic of the night."

"After a long discussion with our Asian partners it has come to our attention of some faulty maneuvering from some players within the organization," he continued as he readied a drink and turned on classical music.

Almost instantaneously a couple of men were overpowered and brought to the front alongside Don Pacho. The struggling men were indeed some very important members overseeing the large Vancouver area.

"Shut up!" yelled Don Pacho as the men tried to deny any wrong doing and simultaneously were brought down to their knees.

"Gentlemen," Don Pacho addressed all in attendance. "These two men have not been 100% transparent and loyal to the organization."

"We have had very clear guidelines, processes and expectations for anyone that is allowed in," he emphasized.

"If we are to maintain the power and control worldwide," he added as he slipped on a pair of rubber gloves. "We are to keep this magnificently well-oiled machine pure at all times."

Don Pacho proceeded to force feed the drink that he had prepared to one of the men while his hands were tied behind his back and duct tape was placed over his mouth. I can only assume that it was some sort of chemical or acid due to the great struggle and grunting that went on for a few minutes until he laid there lifeless.

Don Pacho removed his gloves and disposed of them as the second man remained on his knees with his hands also tied behind his back. Instead of getting a second glass he opened a drawer from a nearby table and took out a handgun. As the man pleaded for his life, confessing to some bad choices, Don Pacho proceeded to put on a silencer on the gun without a saying a word to this soon-to-be-dead man.

"Juancho!" Don Pacho said firmly. "Come here."

My heart had already been racing as I witnessed all of this before my eyes. Having experienced what went down in Sincelejo did not prepare me for this in any measure. I discarded the possibility of this being an April Fool's joke because it was clear that he wanted me to kill this guy; he handed me the gun and took a couple of steps back.

I hesitated even pointing the gun at this man. I looked back at Don Pacho feeling sweat down my back and my forehead. I could feel and hear my heavy breathing. The gun felt like it weighed a thousand pounds. I couldn't even hear the man pleading anymore; it's as if time stood still.

"Juancho, do it for your family," Don Pacho whispered as I maintained eye contact with him and pulled the trigger.

I handed the gun back to Don Pacho without even looking at the body and returned to my seat.

After the meeting I found one of the many bathrooms and locked myself in for what felt like an eternity. I washed my face hoping to wake up from the nightmare I had gotten myself into and only seemed to get worse with time. I dried myself and stared into my eyes trying to get my thoughts straight. Who had I become? I had just taken a life. The whole experience of taking down a whole helicopter back in Colombia still seemed too surreal to actually affect me, but this, this was different.

We would be spending the night here with an early flight back to Miami so I took a guest room knowing very well that there wouldn't be any sleep with what I had just done. I looked at my phone and I was surprised to see a text from Brooke; I missed being in her arms.

'Juan, we love you, remember who you are!'

Who was I? I felt like it was impossible to know exactly at this moment. I've never been around so many people and felt so alone at the same time in my life. Since the flight back from Dubai I've had a continuous mix of emotions or feelings; an odd combination between doubt and resolution. Doubt because I feel that no matter how things move forward, it won't end well on both ends. Resolution because I know what I'm going to do; I just need the way to make it happen. However, I feel that the resolution can only feed the doubt at this point.

Back at home I tried to shake off what had happened just a few days ago by immersing myself fully in my role as family man. No expected trips with Don Pacho were on my calendar for the next couple of weeks; the only trip being my meet-up with Neal in Boston at the end of this week. Brooke seemed to be moving along with her recovery which meant dressing up a little and going out as husband and wife despite only being two and a half weeks since she gave birth to little Rocky. During dinner she probed for details about the Vancouver trip, which I gladly had prepared for before today - just in case it came up again.

The week moved along with some more investments starting with the purchase of a few vacation homes. We purchased a $6.5 million beach home in Mission Beach in the San Diego area followed by a $5 million beach home in Newport Beach. Next we acquired a luxury townhome in Park City, Utah for $3.9 million and ended the shopping spree with a beach home in Costa Rica and a luxury penthouse in Medellin. Not a bad way to add to your business portfolio.

FRIDAY APRIL 1ST, 2016 – BOSTON, MA

On Friday I took Don Pacho's jet to Boston to avoid any suspicion. I thought about just flying out there myself but I had been using his jet this whole time so it would be odd if I didn't. In addition to that, Don Pacho had recently received a special delivery; his new Brabus private jet all the way from Germany. I might as well call this my jet now.

On our way there I sent a text to Neal to confirm our dinner appointment later tonight. My plan was to discuss the "script" that I was working on and the specific help I would need from him. He surprised me with a change of plans; he wanted to invite me to his home where his wife would prepare a special meal for us tonight. Neal offered to pick me up from Logan International and took on the role of tour guide as we drove past the downtown area and into his neck of the woods, Back Bay.

"Juan, do you like baseball?" asked an excited Neal as we rolled to a red light.

"I never been into baseball," I replied, "I play soccer."

"Why do you ask?" I added.

"Oh, we live a few blocks away from Fenway Park," he answered. "I never was into baseball but we got into it when we moved here."

"We're Red Sox fans now by default I guess," He chuckled.

"I've actually never been to a major league baseball game," I replied.

"Do you wanna go tomorrow?" he asked as we looked for an open parking spot.

"I don't want to impose Neal," I answered.

"Oh, you wouldn't be, it would be our pleasure to take you as our guest!" he continued. "You would think that spending a few million dollars in your home would at least come with a good parking spot."

We had to go around the block a couple of times until we could find a spot a few houses down from his on Marlborough St. In the meantime he explained to me that his daily commute compensated for the pain of parking each day. MIT was directly across the Charles River from Back Bay; still a 20 minute drive due to traffic going across the Harvard Bridge into the school.

"Is finding a spot always like this?" I asked as he paralleled park his Jaguar.

"I would be lying if I said no," he answered.

Neal's wife, Marci, prepared a wonderful dinner with help from their personal chef. We were able to talk for a couple of hours about many things; not being able to discuss the main topic of the night however. After the 3-course meal we were finally able to talk about my script so we walked up to their terrace to have a chat.

"Juan would you like a cup of coffee?" offered Neal as he turned on a couple of outdoor heaters. "It's still a little bit chilly but it should warm up soon."

"No, thank you," I answered. "I don't drink coffee."

"Alright, so tell me about this project you're working on," he said. "It sounds exciting."

I honestly think I might have a story for a book or movie with all the stuff I came up with. I needed it to sound like a real story and I was able to come up with one during the flight. Neal said that he liked it so he told me that my character could go a couple of ways about using chemistry to kill the antagonist. The first thing he brought up was using a chemical called Potassium Chloride. When given, the drug simply is metabolized into potassium and chloride ions, both of these ions are normally already in the human body. He said that Potassium is already an important mineral for the proper functioning of all cells, tissues and organs in the human body; particularly for nerves and muscles. It also helps in maintaining proper blood pressure and pH of body fluids; Don Pacho has low blood pressure. However, when potassium chloride is injected in the body in excess quantities, it can cause kidney failure, sudden cardiac arrest and ultimately in the death of that person. Important side note, the medical examiner will not get the actual reason behind high potassium levels in the blood.

For the next couple of hours Neal shared with me some interesting ideas but all of them would require the help from someone else to get it done and that's just too risky for me. He listed a few options in the likes of Ricin; like it was portrayed by Walter White on Breaking Bad. Tetrodotoxin, which is found in certain parts of the Pufferfish body but unfortunately Don Pacho is not a fan of sushi. Another one was Saxitoxin, which apparently was researched by the CIA in the 1960's. It accumulates in shellfish and can occasionally cause food poisoning which can result in paralysis and respiratory failure. Aside from Ricin I don't see how I could incorporate any of these into my plan.

The last one that Neal brought up did grab my attention; using Botulinum. Botulinum is a very powerful nerve agent that is typically used in small quantities for general anti-aging treatments; lo and behold, it is better known as "Botox". Don Pacho is an avid user of Botox. However, the main problem is still present with this route; I would still need a second person to be part of this. He did introduce me once to the person that has been injecting him with Botox for the last decade or so; the problem there is that they're good friends.

Saturday morning I dropped by our Boston carwash so I could at least say I had been there. In addition to that I was able to attend the Boston Red Sox game along with Neal and his wife. During the game I talked to Neal about the carwash and the chemicals that were being used and any possible recommendations so we could go green. All this was just to have content to give Don Pacho about my trip up here.

After Neal and Marci dropped me off at the airport I received a text from Don Pacho notifying me about a last minute meeting tomorrow evening. The meeting would take place in Don Pacho's private suite at the American Airlines Arena for the Miami/Orlando game. He didn't specify who the meeting was with but I can only hope it's not as intense as last time's meeting.

SUNDAY APRIL 3RD, 2016 – MIAMI, FL

Sunday lunch was spent indoors with Brooke and the boys due to the heavy rain. Things between Brooke and me felt normal once again until she made the comment about how she had made a couple's therapy appointment for this Wednesday. To avoid an argument we decided to come back to that later.

After putting the boys down for a nap I joined Brooke in our bed.

"Couple's therapy," I repeated in unbelief, "Why?"

"Juan, it's obvious that you and I need to work on our marriage," she responded. "Well, if you want to of course."

"I think we need professional help if we want to stay married," She emphasized.

"Professional help, are you serious?" I asked perplexed. "Since when do we need professional help?"

"Juan, you've changed since you started working with your boss," she explained. "You don't include me in your decisions and barely talk to me anymore; I feel like there's an invisible barrier between us."

"Not to mention the danger that you've put yourself and all of us in by being with someone like him," She added without having the slightest clue how bad it really was.

"Will you please come with me?" she pleaded.

"Yes, I will," I conceded as I took her in my arms to console her.

I love my wife and my family. I really do believe that I have the perfect family and I have only wanted the best for them. I admit that along the way I have made some poor decisions; some have transformed into monumental obstacles but since the damage has already been done, all I can focus on now is fixing the problem. After some "reconciliation" I told

Brooke that I would be attending the Miami Heat game later today with Don Pacho and some "investors."

I thought it was better to refer to them as such rather than associates. Brooke had me promise her to be more open about my meetings, trips and whereabouts.

On the drive to the arena I contemplated on possible ways of using the Botox option in my plan. Using his Botox guy was definitely out of the question; I would have to find another scenario for Don Pacho to get his Botox - possibly in a different setting. As I was parking the Tumbler, it dawned on me that he had to get his Botox fix somehow when he was out of town for an extended period of time. That was it; I had to get him out of town to get him an overdose of Botox. It would have to be in a smaller town maybe in the Caribbean; I would think that getting a Botox treatment in a bigger city the doctors would be more cautious to avoid any type of future lawsuit. I would still need a second person to move forward with my plan but I would assume that it's much easier to pay someone off.

Once I made my way up to the suite Don Pacho introduced me to the group of men in attendance; his guests for the night. He had flown them in from several parts of the world. He explained to me that between these men they controlled 78% of the Indian market. The majority stake was controlled by the Russian mafia, primarily in the Goa region in the south west of India. They were by far the most numerous and influential organized crime organization in the country without leaving out the fact that they owned the police force thus giving them free reign everywhere. Also in attendance were Israeli and Nigerian drug lords, making this meeting a pivotal milestone since none of our friends in the Golden Triangle had ever been successful in meeting with them without ending in a blood bath.

Don Pacho wanted to work out a truce with them and discuss the possibility of working together to maximize revenue from the Indian market and neighboring areas. If anyone can accomplish this impossible partnership it would definitely be Don Pacho. The worst-case scenario is that they say no and Don Pacho simply wipes them out; he never takes no for an answer after all. The meeting continued well into the game and I was not surprised to see these men decline the offer; if only they knew who they were saying no to. They did agree to a truce between the sides but were still reluctant to working together. For a minute I thought to myself that Don Pacho was keeping his cool and taking a no for the first time since I met him; I was wrong. He simply pulled out his little black pocket book and made some notes.

The post-game festivities consisted of drinks aboard Don Pacho's yacht. He said that the truce needed to be celebrated and what better way to do it than in South Beach style.

"Juancho, I will see you tomorrow," Don Pacho said as we made our way down to the cars.

"Oh, I can stay if you want me to," I responded.

"Don't worry my friend," he continued. "Go take care of your family."

"Seriously Don Pacho, I can stay," I replied.

"Juancho, go take care of your family!" he repeated. "I insist."

I got the message loud and clear. I don't know what I was thinking; he did use his pocket book after all so he obviously didn't want me present.

On my way home I made a quick stop at the supermarket for some ice cream wanting to surprise the boys. At home I walked into an unusually quiet home and quickly realized that it was past 10 p.m. already; the boys had been in bed for a while now. Brooke and I ended the night together watching her favorite movie, Couple's Retreat, in our home theater.

MONDAY APRIL 4TH, 2016

The morning commute was horrendous on my way to the office - not that it was ever a treat but it hadn't been this bad for a while. As I inched my way closer to the downtown area I noticed an unusual amount of police cars, ambulances, helicopters and news vans everywhere I looked. I didn't think of turning on the radio but once I made it up to my office I had an unobstructed view of the area where all these first responders were concentrated. Something big had happened in the bay, which made me think of the one person that most likely was behind this - Don Pacho. I wonder what crazy crap he did now. The man was completely unpredictable and creative to say the least.

As soon as I turned on my TV the first thing that I heard from the reporter was that they had ruled out terrorism. The next channel seemed to have more information; they mentioned that the authorities had begun looking into a possible drug related war - Bingo. I changed the channel one more time to see if I could get more about the actual event. The newscaster explained that witnesses in the area had seen a luxury yacht in the middle of the bay at around midnight last night shortly before an explosion was seen and heard throughout the Miami downtown area. According to the report authorities had not given an official body count but did confirm that there had not been any survivors from the yacht and multiple minor injuries caused by chattered glass around a mile radius.

I was pretty shocked that Don Pacho decided to use his own yacht; it was definitely one of his favorite toys. Almost simultaneously, the TV said that the yacht was registered to a Miami Heat player but reported stolen earlier in the day; that made more sense.

To say that Don Pacho is a mad man is a complete understatement; the man may not be as bloodthirsty as he was in the 80s and 90s, but he remains just as lethal in every sense of the word. A human being like that will definitely not be missed once he's finally gone; it would be a public disservice not to kill him.

With this "wise" move from Don Pacho I would think that there would be consequences when you mess with the Russian mafia and much more when you blow up their leaders. Yes, Don Pacho is much more powerful than them but the mafia is the mafia and I'm sure they won't just back off. Now I have to include the Russian mafia as one of my problems by default. Then again, maybe I can make lemonade out of lemons from this situation; they could get to him before I make any type of move on him. However, I am Don Pacho's right hand man making me a target as well if or when they decide to retaliate.

Damn you Don Pacho!

Today was just full of surprises; Brooke texted me that the Haight's had invited us over to The Biltmore Hotel for a whole day event. However, because of the boys one of us would have to stay home to watch them. Brooke insisted that I would go first and hang out with Bruce this coming Saturday. In a way to convince me she listed all the amenities of The Biltmore as if she had forgotten that I didn't even like golf, I was not a fan of spas; in fact, I didn't like anyone else touching me and finally the most important one, I did not want to hang out with the Director of the DEA. She finally used the 'We need adult friends' card and I just couldn't fight her on it any longer.

On Wednesday I got a call from the local Mercedes Benz dealership telling me that they had my new custom car ready for pick-up. I dropped it off at MC Customs the same day for some work on it. On Thursday, Brooke was visited by an armored vehicle here at home delivering her new earrings. Later that day, Rocky had his first checkup at his pediatrician; I think the first month shots hurt me more than they did Rocky. On Friday I came across yet another business opportunity back in Utah. Brooke's dad informed us that our former gym - Treehouse Athletic Club - had been put up for sale this past week. I called the same day and placed a bid.

SATURDAY APRIL 9TH, 2016

The dreaded day finally came. Bruce picked me up at 8 a.m. in his DEA-issued SUV; identical to the SUVs that had pulled me over some time ago. I was definitely not looking forward to the chitchat that was going to unfold throughout the day; it would be forced and unnatural. I purposefully made a constant effort to keep the conversation away from business as we ate breakfast and played a couple of rounds of golf. Prior to lunch we made our way to a half full steam room where we finally had some much needed silence.

It must have been my constant redirecting of questions throughout the day that got him talking a lot more about him, his family and his professional background. I actually began to believe and most importantly, feel that I could indeed trust him. I don't know if it was because he was a family man or based on the stories he told me about his rough upbringing in the south.

My situation was complex and it wouldn't hurt to have an ally. Now the problem was finding the best way to open up about all this. There must have been some telepathic connection between us because as I was about to break the silence he chimed in with a question that helped pave the way for the rest of the conversation.

"Juan, can I ask you a personal question?" he asked as the last person walked out of the steam room leaving us alone.

"Yes Bruce, shoot!" I replied as I listened intently to the sound of his voice unable to see his expression through the steam.

"Are you and your family in any type of danger?" he asked.

His question caught me a little off guard.

"Excuse me?" I replied.

"From the moment we met and our very limited interactions until today," he explained, "I have been able to perceive that you are a genuine good guy; one of the few I've met in the last few years."

"It boggles my mind as to why you would be working for someone like your boss," he added. "That is unless you have something to lose."

I couldn't have asked for a more perfect scenario and place for me to share my current situation. It helped ease my paranoia about Don Pacho spying on me or listening in to my conversations.

"Bruce, I don't know where to begin," I answered as I felt my heart race. "I work for a very powerful and dangerous man."

"You wouldn't believe me if I told you the things I have seen and come to know in the last year," I added.

"Try me," He responded.

"Ok, here it goes, I work for Pablo Escobar," I hesitated but to my surprise there was no response from Bruce.

"He has been alive for the last two decades," I continued as my voice echoed in the small steam room.

I began at the condo fire and explained thoroughly how I came to know this unbelievable piece of information. I briefly went through the many excavation trips around the world leaving out the exact amount that was buried. I talked about the content of the meetings in Germany, Spain, Las Vegas, Vancouver and here in Miami. After a while Bruce finally spoke up saying that despite whether Don Pacho was really who I said he was, one thing for sure is that we are in real danger.

"I have always known that he was a drug trafficker," he exclaimed. "He always manages to slide through our fingers."

"Let me ask you this," he added, "Have you thought about what you're going to do?"

"Based on what you've told me, it seems that he has eyes and ears on your whole family," he continued. "Practically making it impossible to run away and hide."

"I do or at least I think I do," I responded. "I need to take care of him."

"Just to make sure that we're on the same page," he clarified. "You're talking about killing him, am I right?"

"Yes, I am," I replied.

"May I ask 'how' you're planning on executing that?" he asked.

I was surprised that his immediate reaction wasn't what I would expect someone in law enforcement would initially have.

"There are a few possibilities but I think I've narrowed it down to a Botox overdose," I answered.

"So using a large dose of Botulinum then?" he asked.

"Yes, do you know much about it?" I replied surprised.

"I'm not, but my wife is a big fan of it," he chuckled. "I guess it's a 'Must' for many in our neighborhood."

"Wouldn't you agree Juan?" he added jokingly.

"I guess my next question would be how you would go about doing it?" he asked.

"That's where I'm stuck," I replied. "It can't be stateside so I would have to look into getting him out of the country."

"Hmm….the challenge in my opinion is finding a place where he would feel comfortable doing it outside of his usual place," he explained, "but also having a person executing it without a hitch."

"I agree," I answered bemused, he agreed with what I had just shared.

"We could possibly have one of our agents be that person," he added.

"Does the DEA have jurisdiction outside of the US?" I asked while literally answering my own question, "What am I saying; the DEA is all over the globe right?" I chuckled.

"I do need to ask," I said. "If what I'm claiming is correct about this being Pablo Escobar, wouldn't you want to catch him alive to prosecute him?"

"On paper, yes, but if it's really him," he explained. "That would open a whole can of worms."

"That would mean that his death was staged back in '93 and that he had, or most likely still has, people working for him in the DEA in addition to the many other organizations and governments," he noted.

"Or he faked his own death," I chimed in. "He could've had a body double."

"True, but we can't run the risk of bringing up something like this not knowing who to trust," he emphasized.

"The safe way to go about it would be to disregard that possibility and apprehend him just as he is today," he said.

"He is after all a powerful and dangerous drug dealer, whether it's Escobar or not," He chuckled. "Bringing in a man like that to justice is always a good thing on a resume."

"Or we can just kill him," I added as the sauna door opened and in came a group of men.

After the sauna we made our way to Fontana Italian restaurant at the ground level of the hotel. As the host led us to our table, Bruce chose a different table alongside the large water fountain. Once I sat down he quickly stood up again. He said that if I didn't mind he would rather sit facing the other way. As we changed seats I noticed that he had left a note near my napkin with a message written on top.

"Do not read here, open at home."

During our late lunch we continued with a light conversation about my different business ventures here in Miami and back in Utah. In case someone was indeed checking us out, I didn't want to make it obvious that I was putting a note in my pocket so I casually covered it with my phone for the remainder of the meal.

Once behind the security of extra dark tinted windows in my new ride I felt safe enough to open the note. Bruce began by stating the obvious; that I was most likely being followed so it would be better to keep our distance from each other. He advised me to become a member of the club and to make it a habit to spend a couple of days here; he would leave me a note strategically hidden as a means of communication. I would do the same in return.

The next step would be up to me; I would have to come up with the where and when for this operation. In other words I would have to create the opportunity, which entails finding the location, which can't be an unusual place, so I can then inform the DEA and they can prepare accordingly.

On the drive home I stopped behind a car at a red light; I noticed that it had a personalized license plate saying Bor1cua with a 1 instead of an 'I'.

What caught my attention and got me thinking was the license plate frame; it had a Puerto Rican flag.

Puerto Rico

My mind took off with a possible plan.

What if I bought or invested in a clinic in Puerto Rico that specialized in Botox treatments? It was definitely a random way to come up with a plan but it may just work so I'll take it. Now the next thing would be the 'why' and 'how' to get Don Pacho to go completely out of his way for a Botox treatment?

At home I was able to spend some time with the family before dinner and bath time. Brooke and I enjoyed another movie in our home theater and once she called it a night I decided to do some online searches for beauty salons, beauty clinics and medical clinics in and near San Juan.

The next morning I called my mom before everyone was up to ask her about a friend of hers that is from Puerto Rico; I asked her to find out if this friend knew of anyone that either owned or was wanting to start a clinic themselves. By the end of the day my mom already had an answer for me; her friend had been playing with the idea of starting a business in Puerto Rico with a few of her friends that lived on the island. All of them had more than 20 years of experience in these types of services collectively so the last piece of the puzzle was to find someone with the capital; this could work.

I asked my mom to set up a meeting with her for this coming Wednesday or Thursday; I would fly out there for this meeting but also to close the *Treehouse* deal. I was the owner of a gym now since they accepted my offer to sell; they got back to me yesterday afternoon. The other thing that I wanted to do while I was in Utah was to look at available lots to build a custom home in the Draper area. I wanted to build a house plan that I've had for a long time saved in my laptop and I might as well build it so we could retire there; my Florida days are sort of numbered now.

Sunday evening we joined most of our neighbors at a neighborhood barbecue; it was hosted by the wives of the Telemundo anchor and the novelist that lived down the street from us and next door to Bruce's house. I needed to tell Bruce of the plan that I was coming up with but I had to follow his advice for communication; I opted for a small note telling him where I would leave the bigger note. My wife gravitated towards Mallory right from the moment we walked through the door; so much for keeping my distance from Bruce. At one point I offered to get everyone a drink; the girls were good so I got Bruce a drink. I took the opportunity to place the note under the cup as I handed him the drink. The note specified that I would be leaving the note taped under the bench in the same section of the locker room as last time. I walked over to the inflatable jungle gym in the backyard to ask Christian David if he was hungry. While I was trying to get Christian David to come to me, I was approached by a new face.

"It's practically impossible to get the kids out of that thing and get them to eat," he chuckled. "I don't know why my wife orders these things."

"Hi, my name is John," he smiled. "John Lund; I was going to say that this is my party but to tell you the truth I didn't have anything to do with the planning."

"That's not true," I replied. "You must be the one paying for it."

"Very true," he laughed, "very good observation."

"I've been travelling too much around the country promoting a couple of books," he explained. "So I've never had the opportunity to meet you."

"You and your family are fairly new in the neighborhood, am I right?" he added.

John was the novelist. He had one of the largest homes in the neighborhood so we naturally talked about his profession. He explained to me that most of his books were published under various names, never his own, hence the 'John Lund' never appearing on the cover of a novel.

"I love writing Crime Thrillers," he explained. "There's just something about letting your mind run wild with a subject that tends to fascinate readers so much."

"You know Juan," he whispered. "I think everyone has a story to tell."

"Anyone could write a novel, whether it be based on truth or 100% fiction," he added.

I think he has a point. I bet my story would be based on my many 'adventures' and readers would definitely think that it was fiction; no way that these things could happen to a regular person. I guess I could pull a "Jordan Belfort" with my story; from unbelievably crazy lifestyle to a book and then to a movie. Martin Scorsese and my story would be a definite Oscar for best novel adaptation for sure; something to think about I guess.

WEDNESDAY JUNE 22ND, 2016

A month and a half flew by since my initial meeting with my mom's friend, Gloria, about opening the new medical clinic in Puerto Rico. I sat down with her and we had a conference call right there in the restaurant; we met with her friends that would be part of this new business venture. I have left all of the planning and foot work to the ladies since they know what they're doing. Based on our last conference call, we are looking at a July 2016 opening; shooting for Friday the 1st in nine days. My communication with Bruce has continued as planned and according to him the DEA is ready to go once I give them the green light. The plan at this point is to go through with the opening and everything that comes along with a ribbon cutting. We'll let the clinic settle in within the community and in the first week of August we'll roll out our plan, which consists of having a female DEA agent play the part of an employee. Bruce said that to cover all our bases we should have this female agent begin work at the clinic as soon as we open the doors. Being the main investor in this, I will have to put her in since my associates are not planning on hiring any outside applicants.

I was also able to find a prime piece of land for my custom home. I met with Lane Myers Construction in Draper and had them begin the process of building on a four acre lot in the Steeplechase community. On a nostalgic note, when I was working on my undergraduate degree at the University of Utah I remember visualizing my home in this neighborhood some day; the law of attraction at its best. I never thought that wealth would come in the form it has but I had to adapt to it. The house will be ready by Christmas; we'll be spending the holidays in Utah again but this time in our new corner canyon mansion with an awesome view of the Salt

Lake Valley. The other meeting I had that week was to close the *Treehouse* deal which is yet more evidence of the law of attraction in full display.

Without getting too ahead of myself, we also had other important milestones worthy to mention. Back in April, we had the opportunity of having the first dance production/performance under Brooke's ownership of the studio. A few days following the production I got to meet with the twins at the studio to discuss katieandkellie rompers and any updates from the last time we met. We had my in-laws and my parents over for two weeks for a mini vacation to Disney World. I talked business with my dad about the possibility of adding a few more locations for his current franchises; our business empire was beginning to look like a heavyweight contender with a hefty portfolio.

In early June I had a couple of trips; the first one with stops in Hong Kong and Shanghai. We were merging with a fish food company with huge operations in these two cities; the merger came with a $50 million price tag. According to Don Pacho his motive for the merger had no ties to the "illegal" side of his business ventures, in his words it was a "good business move."

My second trip was to New Orleans; the first time returning after living here between '04 and '06. The purpose this time around was very different than 10 years ago. We had a 50-ton shipment of flour come in through the Big Easy from the Middle East. The shipment contained flour but it was creatively mixed with cocaine which our chemists later separated in our labs. The street value of this shipment once it hit the streets would be in the billions of dollars. The monstrous profit is now split only between Don Pacho and our associates in Asia since several main players are out of the picture now. As the greeter and supervisor of this operation, it was my utmost priority to make sure that things moved smoothly once the containers made it to the Port of New Orleans. My compensation would be one percent of the total amount once the shipment was sold in its entirety. However, I would receive the first half up front; that one percent would equal $1 billion.

It didn't take long for Don Pacho to make me a billionaire, even though I won't be seeing my name on any Forbes lists any time soon. They can always come up with new categories; I've seen one for athletes, celebrities and tech geeks. Forbes could make a custom category for criminals that could include pharmaceutical companies, politicians and drug traffickers – but I wouldn't hold my breath.

Before heading home I stopped at Don Pacho's humble abode; he had texted me earlier in the day at the office. We talked Canada and how starting next week we would begin intensifying our distribution efforts using all the Canadian cities that were on the board in the Vancouver meeting. He needed me in Vancouver this coming Monday to welcome yet another 50-ton shipment of flour; another billion dollar payday for me. After completing this assignment, my net worth will have grown two billion dollars in a matter of weeks. On my way out I decided to invite Don Pacho to the Grand Opening of the clinic the Friday after I returned from Canada.

"Definitely Juancho, I could even be your first customer," he said. "I can get my Botox fix a week early."

"I'm sure my Botox guy won't mind," he added.

This changed things, at least in my opinion. We could definitely move up the plan from August to now but I would have to run it by Bruce in this Saturday's note.

Back at home I reheated the food that Stefan, our chef, had made for dinner. I played with the boys a little bit before helping Brooke give them a bath and put them to bed. She then sprung a surprise on me.

"Juan, the boys and I will be flying out to Utah this Saturday," she said as she brushed her hair on our bed. "We'll be back on July 2."

"When did you decide on a week-long trip?" I asked a little surprised at the random news.

"Today, my brother is heading to medical school," she explained. "And my parents are giving him a sort-of farewell."

"Ok, can I at least take you guys to the airport?" I asked a little annoyed.

I could sense that Brooke was upset; she never got back to her own happy self since that one talk when she gave me the ultimatum. She obviously was using her brother as an excuse to be away from me; so be it.

We had a beach day on Friday since I wouldn't be able to be with them for a whole week. On another note, the random moment of the day went to a reported shark attack as we were picking up our things to leave.

SATURDAY JUNE 25TH, 2016

I was able to send off Brooke and the boys in Don Pacho's jet this afternoon before making my way to the resort. I was missing Rocky's first plane ride. Bruce and I had planned for him to spend the first part of the day at the club and then I would head there later in the day. On the way there I decided to stop at Panpaya Latin Grill in the mall so I wouldn't have to spend a ridiculous amount of money for lunch. Yes, I was now a billionaire with a $2.6 billion net worth and rising, but that didn't mean I was willing to spend unjustifiable amounts of money, especially on overpriced food.

As I made it to The Biltmore, I was unable to pull up to the curb for the valet to take my car. The whole curb was taken by police cars, an ambulance and a forensics truck. Something bad had happened and I instantly had a sick feeling in my stomach. I took my gym bag out of the trunk and made my way in. The lobby seemed to have all the hotel guests in clusters trying to get a glimpse of what had happened. As I got closer to the spa area I was stopped by a police officer and asked to stay on my side of the police tape. On the opposite side of the lobby I could see another police officer talking with a member of the staff; I think it was a towel boy that I had seen before. After a good 20 minutes the boy walked out one of the side doors so I followed him and caught up to him as he was getting in his car.

"Excuse me," I called out. "I noticed you were giving your report to an officer."

"What happened?" I asked as I could see that he was pretty shaken.

"I walked in...he was dead," he tried to answer me holding back tears, "so much blood."

"I'm sorry, I'm sure it must be hard to talk about it," I tried to comfort him. "But did you recognize the victim?"

"Yes," he whispered. "It was Mr. Haight."

"Haight, Bruce Haight?" I asked in unbelief.

"Yes," he answered as he shut the car door and sped off.

I felt sick. I sat on the curb with my hands covering my face for a few minutes, or hours- I'm not sure. I thought we had been careful during this whole time. There was no other explanation for this, the bastard had killed him! All I could think about was his wife and kids. He had been the closest thing to a friend, an ally, to me in all of this. How the hell was I going to get the information over to the DEA now?

I decided to drive back home since there was no point in staying. I was never going to be able to get into that locker room to get Bruce's last note from under the bench. By the time that the crime scene was cleaned up, the note would most likely be gone as well. Another reason to worry about now is if Bruce's hitman got to the note; that would not be good at all. On Sunday morning I called reception to ask if the spa would be open at all. I was told that the resort would be open as normal since the crime scene had been cleared. I made it to the resort and was able to breathe again once I saw the note still in its place. On my way out I asked a member of the staff about the event and I was told that apparently Bruce's body had been found in one of the showers. She went well into detail about how the body was found; not that I had asked.

As I pulled in to our neighborhood a good 20 cars covered both sides of the street; visitors at Bruce's house consoling Mallory and the kids most likely. As I backed my car into the garage, a thought came out of the blue; killing Don Pacho was not only for my family's safety anymore, I would also be doing it for Bruce and his family.

I was only able to spend a few hours at home before having to leave again to Vancouver in Don Pacho's new Brabus jet; Brooke had taken the other plane. All the money in the world didn't matter at this point; I was not in the celebrating mood. The ugly side of this industry was becoming more prevalent. The frightening thought was that it could only get worse from here on out. With a little bit of luck on my side I would only have to wait until the end of this week to eliminate all danger to my family.

Once I returned from Vancouver I hated going home to an empty house so I took advantage of the available time and played soccer every day. It got me out of the house and it helped me with the increasing stress at the same time. As the week rolled on I began having an odd feeling all the time, not necessarily a sick feeling, but definitely not a good feeling. It could be due to the nerves about Puerto Rico, but my mind was also preoccupied thinking about Brooke and our relationship. I felt as if my family was slowly deteriorating; if only Brooke could understand that all this is for the best of the family. I hope that after all this blows over, she can finally understand and forgive me.

Thursday night I spent completely awake. The nerves completely kicked in about what exactly was going to go down the following morning. If things moved forward according to plan, not only would my family's future be secured, but I would be the man who finally took down Pablo Escobar. The world and history books would never know, but I would and that's good enough for me. One thing that I do wonder is what will happen to all of his money, businesses and real estate?

FRIDAY JULY 1ST, 2016 – SAN JUAN, PR

We made it to San Juan in a quick two and a half hour flight. As always 'La Isla del Encanto' has the perfect weather, people, music and electric vibe. A white Bentley Convertible was already there for our stay since Puerto Rico was one of the few places where Don Pacho did not have a personal driver waiting for his every command. Leaving the airport our British navigation spoke over the Merengue music to tell us the quickest way to Guaynabo where we had decided to open the clinic. We crossed over Laguna San Jose on the Teodoro Moscoso Bridge which reminded me so much of my time driving on the Lake Pontchartrain Causeway in New Orleans. As we turned onto Avenida San Patricio Don Pacho pointed at a cluster of trees and said that a friend of his owned a multi-million dollar home inside the gated community just over the group of trees.

"We should drop by after the Grand Opening and surprise him." He said as we pulled into an open parking spot right in front of the clinic that was reserved for me.

Despite being a huge mess of nerves inside, I agreed with him as confidently as possible.

"I love the area Juancho," said Don Pacho as he took off his designer sunglasses.

Guaynabo had some of the most expensive commercial real estate on the island, but we decided that the demographic that we wanted to target already gravitated towards that area.

"I would've picked the exact same spot," he added as he pulled out a cigar.

I thought about telling him that he couldn't smoke inside but it's his last cigar after all; he can have it.

The ladies welcomed us inside to the large beautifully-decorated waiting area already full at capacity with potential new customers and neighboring businesses. We definitely had not held back with the expenses for the clinic and the Grand Opening. The event resembled an after party for an awards ceremony with all the beautiful people dressed to impress. The ladies and I wanted to make this clinic the most exclusive and coveted place for all-things-beauty. I was introduced to many local important people in government, entertainment, models and wealthy neighbors.

All of this was fun but I could've done without most of it since all this was just a show to convince the real guest of the hour, Don Pacho. Towards the end of the 3-hour event, a beautiful girl in a shiny blue gown walked up to me as I was getting a drink.

"Mr. Arias, great party," she said.

"I just wanted to make sure that you knew how grateful I am for the job," she continued.

"You're welcome," I replied. "And you are?"

"Oh," I added as she didn't answer and continued to smile at me.

It took me a second to realize that she was the DEA agent that Bruce had assigned for the job. I wasn't expecting such an attractive girl to be working for the DEA and especially for an assignment like this.

"Juancho, the clinic seems to be a hit with the locals," Don Pacho chuckled as he prepared himself a drink as the girl walked away.

"Be careful with the girls, it gets easier each time," he added.

"Brooke has nothing to worry about," I answered. "She works here."

"In fact, she will be the one giving you the Botox treatment after the party," I added.

As I wrapped up the event from the stage I thanked everyone for their attendance and support. As I added a few more words we had several of our models walk around handing party gifts out to the more than 200 attendees. The Grand Opening had been a total success, but the real success was yet to come. As the cleaning crews began the clean-up effort Don Pacho followed Isabel, the DEA agent, to one of the available rooms.

"Juancho, you're coming with me right?" Don Pacho laughed. "I want to have a witness in case there's any kind of sexual harassment towards me."

After closing the door behind me I decided to sit on the leather love seat across from him.

"Juancho, you're sweating pretty badly," he pointed out as he lay back on his chair. "The party is over, take off your coat."

I was sweating pretty profusely but it was not because of the coat. I proceeded to take off my coat but remained standing. My hands were freezing; the only sign I've been told to have when I'm nervous. I rested on the sink and crossed my arms as I watched intently as the syringe was finally prepared. Isabel was just about to give the injection when she stopped herself and said that she needed to use another one; she didn't explain why.

"Not a fan of shots Juancho?" Don Pacho chuckled.

"You should look at your face right now." he added as I smiled somewhat nervously.

What the hell is taking her so long? It's as if she's prolonging the whole thing. Just do it already!

She carefully placed her left hand on Don Pacho's forehead and slowly picked up the syringe with her other hand.

She was about to place the injection when I suddenly heard commotion outside the room and almost simultaneously the door was kicked in. A group of men ran in decked out in DEA vests holding assault rifles.

"What the hell is the meaning of this!?" I shouted completely surprised as Don Pacho and I were placed in handcuffs.

This is why she took so long on giving him the injection; the DEA changed the plan on me. Even though my change of plans never made it to Bruce, I'm sure this chick noticed that Don Pacho had made the trip down here with me and quickly alerted everyone. I looked at her but she was playing the *'I'm scared and don't know what's going on'* card. Don Pacho remained quiet as we were escorted out of the room and through the large reception area.

"Juan, what is going on?" asked one of the ladies frantically.

"Don't worry, it must be some kind of misunderstanding," I replied. "Don't worry about me, I'll get it all cleared up."

"Juancho, no need to say anything," Don Pacho advised once we were outside. "I'll take care of it with a simple phone call."

"Not this time buddy," said one of the DEA agents. "This will be the last..."

Suddenly there was a wave of gunfire coming from different directions hitting the guy putting Don Pacho in one of the two DEA vehicles knocking him and Don Pacho down to the curb.

The guy holding me threw me in the back seat of the other SUV and began to return the gunfire. I struggled to climb up and turn around while having both hands behind my back. I was able to close the door with my foot as I heard bullets flying everywhere. I managed to sit up briefly to see Don Pacho stand up and climb into the other bullet proof SUV.

The firefight went on for quite a long time but after a while it stopped and there was complete silence; the silence seemed to last almost as long as the gun fight. I began to hear footsteps walking around the SUV; someone opened my door asking me to turn around in a heavy Russian accent.

It was the Russians.

As I was pulled out I saw the street covered in DEA agents and the Bentley covered in bullet holes. About a dozen Russians driving BMWs split up taking Don Pacho in one car and me in another. I knew that Don Pacho's decision in messing with the Russian mafia could only mean more problems for me. Now I was being kidnapped.

We were flown back to Miami and as soon as we touched down we were blind folded, taking us separate ways again. I was left in the back seat of an SUV for the night in what sounded like a waterside warehouse. As the night went on I began thinking that maybe this was the way I would die; Brooke, the boys and my whole family would never hear back from me or at least know where my body ended up. This was no way to die at all.

SATURDAY JULY 2ND, 2016 – MIAMI, FL

I was slapped awake in the morning to even worse news. I was told by one of the four men keeping me captive that if I didn't comply with them then they would kill my family in front of me. At first I didn't believe their threats but once I heard Brooke's voice over the phone crying as well as the boys crying in the background I began crying. How did they? I was confused.

"Don't worry; we had some of our men waiting for your family at the airport this morning," the man with the phone said.

"Where are they!?" I shouted.

"Calm down, just work with us and you'll see them again," he replied.

"What do you want from me?" I asked.

"We need you to help us get access into your boss' international bank accounts," he explained.

"Why would I have access to that?" I answered. "I don't."

"Don't lie to us, we know how important you are to your boss," he chuckled. "You have access."

"Where's my boss?" I continued.

"Don't worry about him," He replied.

"Just do what we asked you and you'll be able to see your family today," he added.

"Ok, whatever you want," I answered trying to come up with something.

I told them to head to Don Pacho's house where he kept all that information. I didn't have the slightest clue what I was going to do once we made it there; I needed to come up with something fast.

As we pulled up to Palazzo Napoli I couldn't see any members of the staff; I remembered that Don Pacho had given everyone the weekend off because of the holiday. I wouldn't have any access to the house; my mind raced for the next best thing. As we pulled to a stop I caught a glimpse of Don Pacho's yacht.

"Ok, now what?" asked one of my captors.

"There," I said pointing at the yacht. "He keeps that information in there."

Two of the four men stayed in the SUV while the other two walked me to the yacht. I turned on Don Pacho's laptop; if I remember correctly it's the oldest and slowest computer he has so it could buy me some time. I asked if I could use the bathroom since I had been holding it in for the past 12 hours. They were somewhat reluctant but still allowed me to do so after they made sure there was no way to escape.

Upon finishing my business and washing my hands I remembered Don Pacho saying that you could never protect yourself enough so he had hidden a gun in every room in each of his houses; this rule also included every room of this yacht. I turned the water again and began looking around at possible hiding places. The two thugs had already searched the bathroom and found nothing. I need to think like him. I sat down back on the toilet. If I was Don Pacho and I needed to defend myself quickly I would reach for a gun easily accessible to me. As I extended my arms to see how far I could reach in each direction my eyes locked on a small section on the floor by the sink. Don Pacho had remodeled the entire yacht within the last year and this whole bathroom floor was imported Italian tile; however, this small section seemed to be made with a different material. I touched it and could feel the difference right away.

After putting a little pressure on it I heard a click and it opened just like a middle console in a car. There was the gun with a complimentary silencer; easily accessible to someone on the toilet about to let hell loose on any intruder.

I turned off the water just as one of them knocked on the door ordering me to hurry.

"I'm coming out," I replied and took a couple of deep breaths.

I took one last look at my gun to make sure that the safety was off and I was ready to go. I slowly opened the door just enough to see where they were in the room. In one swift motion I kicked the door to the side and put a bullet in each of them before either of them could turn around. As the sudden rush of adrenaline began to fade one of the phones went off; I looked at the caller ID and it showed a local number. Almost immediately I heard a voice from outside calling for one of these guys and heard footsteps coming my way. I threw myself face down in between both of the bodies lying on top of my gun.

"какого черта!" he yelled.

I heard him walk over towards me, but instead flipped over the body to my left. He continued to speak to himself in Russian as he flipped over the other Russian. The anticipation was killing me. As soon as I felt his foot under me and he flipped me over I sprung around and put a bullet in his head; one more to go.

The fourth guy could walk in any minute wondering where his three buddies were; I peeked out one of the windows and could see that he was still in the SUV. He was the biggest of the 4 men and I wasn't sure if I could take him down by myself. I couldn't kill him since he was the only way to my family's whereabouts. I couldn't just climb out the side either because he could easily see me so I needed to get his attention to get him out of the vehicle. I looked around other rooms for anything that could help me but I was only able to find guns. I didn't have time to look on the second floor of the yacht so I just stopped myself, closed my eyes and took a deep breath. If I were him, where would I hide something more than just a gun, something with more power? Almost immediately I heard a voice say 'Bamboo', or at least I thought I heard a voice. Don Pacho loved to decorate his bedrooms with bamboo so I ran up the stairway to his room. I opened the door to the dormitory and he had four large waist-high ceramic vases imported from Russia; one in each corner with bamboo sticks. I looked inside the first 3 but there was nothing. I walked over to the last one hoping that there was something, but nothing. I sat on the chair next to the last vase; am I going crazy, bamboo?

I stared demoralized at the yachting magazines on top of the glass center table in front of me. Time was running out and I was out of ideas; the only thing I could think of was my family and bamboo. What about bamboo? Almost immediately I focused on the reflection on the glass and I could see more bamboo. I slowly raised my eyes and there was a painting on the wall across from me of bamboo. I stood up and walked over. I looked behind the painting and there was a safe. I put my gun down and quickly removed the painting; it had a keypad for a password. Now what? What could be the password? I used his birth year, name, the word money, the word power; nothing. I rested both of my hands on the wall and closed my eyes again. I again found myself trying to think like him. After about two minutes of silence a series of mental pictures flashed in my mind: Park City, walk-in closet, safe, MiTata61!

I entered 'MiTata61' and heard a click; it was open and inside there was another gun, cash and 3 grenades. I grabbed a grenade and walked over to a window; the last Russian thug was still inside the SUV. I walked over to the cockpit to see if I could find anything for me to use; as I turned around to walk out I was able to find a glass case behind the door with a few M16s in it. I broke the glass and helped myself to one that had a shoulder strap. Once I strapped it on like Rambo I made my way downstairs and climbed out one of the few windows that could be opened port side - alright, moment of truth. I pulled the clip and threw the grenade as far as I could into the water. I climbed in and saw that the grenade had done the job; he was walking over with his gun drawn. I hid behind the bar. As the yelling in Russian got closer I used a silver serving platter as a mirror. As he slowly made his way inside and down the hall I inched my way as well. When I peeked around the corner I noticed that he was pulling out his phone with his other hand, so before he could call reinforcements I walked around the corner and took a shot hitting his hand. He quickly picked up the gun and turned around to take a shot but I was able to take another shot hitting him in the thigh.

"Drop the gun!" I yelled. "Or the next shot is for your head."

He dropped the gun.

I had to hurry, I'm sure that the neighbors had already called the police about the explosion and they would be showing up any minute now. I tried to get information out of him but he was not cooperating. While questioning him I remembered that on the way here the driver had been using the SUV's navigation system; there had to be an address I could use in there. I needed to go and he was just slowing me down so I got rid of the obstacle and put a bullet in his head. I ran to the SUV and yes, there was only one other address. I turned on the SUV, put it in reverse and flipped it around. As I drove down the airstrip of a runway I looked into the rear view mirror and immediately hit the brakes. I stared at Don Pacho's garage; I needed something bigger. I backed up and was able to find an open window in the back. I was going to need his Gurkha truck if I wanted to have a chance against these bastards.

The address was directly south from Star Island on the other side of MacArthur Causeway on Dodge Island - if only I had a boat. On the island I had to drive through the endless maze of containers passing multiple docked cruise liners on my way to the east side of the island. Once the navigation alerted me that I was here all I could see was a white building about a half block away from me with two identical SUVs parked outside; it had to be here, there was nothing else.

With the sun going down already it would be easier to sneak up to the building. I parked Don Pacho's tank behind a container and before I walked over I slipped on the bulletproof vest I had taken from the other SUV. I strapped the M16 around my neck as I climbed on top of some pallets to get a better view through the back. There were only six men guarding Don Pacho but no Brooke and the kids.

Where are they!?

Desperation was beginning to settle in.

If they're not here where else could they be?

At the same time I was thinking of how easy it would be to let these Russians take care of Don Pacho right here tonight. All the trouble that I've gone through with the planning of his death and now the dilemma is that I have to save him if I want to see my family again.

I walked back to the truck completely blank; I would have to pull a 'Sincelejo' again. As I turned on the Ghurka I thought that I could easily ram through the walls with this thing but once inside I'm not sure if I could get Don Pacho out alive. Breaking in would leave me greatly outnumbered so that was out of the question. I suddenly heard a voice again, only this time it said "cell phone". I pulled out the dead Russian's phone out of my pocket and opened the call history; it showed dozens of calls to and from the same number.

I hit dial and waited.

"Vladimir?" asked the voice on the other side.

"Vladimir and his buddies will be dead in the next couple of minutes if you don't bring Don Pacho to me," I answered.

"Let me talk to Vladimir!" he yelled.

"I don't think you get it my friend," I replied. "the only way you'll talk to Vladimir is in person."

"We will be there in a few minutes," he answered.

I wasn't expecting them to comply with my demands that easily, but if I could at least break them up then I would have a better chance of taking them on; I still didn't have a plan.

I saw the main door open and just five of the six men stepped out; no Don Pacho. They opened the back of their SUVs and began prepping their guns. As they all entered their vehicles I heard a voice again.

"Ram them!"

Without thinking twice I hit the gas and T-boned both of them with this tank. The blow was so hard that the first SUV literally flipped over the other one landing upside down about 20 feet away. I stepped out and walked over to the pieces of twisted metal with my M16 drawn. No one could survive a hit like this but just in case we're speaking about exceptionally strong 'Ivan Drago' Russians I decided to shower them with bullets.

I inched my way towards the front door of the warehouse; I opened the door and was immediately welcomed with a couple of bullets that barely missed me. I need to move fast.

"Hey man, I don't want to kill you," I yelled. "I just want my family and make sure that Don Pacho is all right."

"Juancho, I'm all right, just shoot this Russian son of a bitch," he yelled. "It's only the two of us in here."

"It should be an easy kill for you," he added.

"Where are all my men?" he asked.

"Do you want the short answer or the long answer?" I asked sarcastically.

"Short answer is: they're all dead," I explained. "Long answer is: Actually, there is no long answer; they're just dead."

"You're alone," I added.

"Dude, there is no point in wasting any more time," I continued. "I promise there will be no harm to you if you let Don Pacho go and tell me where my wife and kids are."

"Here!" I yelled and threw the M16 inside the warehouse as far as I could.

"I'm coming in," I warned him, "I don't have a gun so please don't shoot me."

I walked inside the poorly lit warehouse with my hands raised and made it about 20 feet in when he ordered me to stop. He had me turn around and get down on my knees. He walked over, searched me and asked me if I had the phone from the other Russian. I told him that it was in my right pocket, as he reached in I heard a loud thud. With my hands still high in the air, I turned around and the guy was face down motionless next to me. Don Pacho had only needed some time unguarded to pick the lock to his handcuffs; team work at its best.

"So much for promising him that no harm would come to him," I chuckled.

"I didn't promise that - you did," Don Pacho answered as he threw away the crowbar.

We tied the motionless Russian to a chair and brought him back to life just in time for some questioning. Just as his Russian counterpart he wasn't too cooperative so after the more physical portion of the questioning we were only able to get unimportant and useless information out of him. We already knew that they were part of the Russian mafia and that they were pissed about us killing their bosses and cutting them out of billions; that was a given. It was only until I lost my patience and went ape shit on him that we finally got something useful. Rage completely took ahold of me and I began smashing his head against every inch of the Mercedes that was parked inside beginning with the passenger side window. After the beating he finally mumbled that my family was being captive inside a suite at the JW Marriott Marquis; the hotel adjacent to our office. Once I confirmed the room number I asked Don Pacho for the gun.

"You said that you would let me live if I told you where your family was," he whispered as he sat up and rested against the side of the car.

"I changed my mind," I replied as I put him out of his misery.

As we walked out towards the Gurkha, I could still hear some groaning coming out of one of the smashed SUVs. Before we left I decided to ram what was left of the vehicles and disposed of them into the water.

"Damn Juancho," Don Pacho said. "The Russians unleashed the beast within you."

Leaving the island Don Pacho placed a call from the Gurkha's satellite phone and ordered that a team be assembled and be prepared to join us within the hour at the hotel. I drove straight to my house to pick up Brooke's SUV since it still had the kids' seats. Don Pacho told me that he was sorry that my family had unfortunately been in the mix of all these problems. According to him, it was never his intention to cause problems to the people that he cared about. I don't know if it's the killing spree I have been on lately but I really want to jump across and feel his last breath of life in my hands.

"Juancho, don't worry," he tried comforting me. "We'll get your family back soon."

At the hotel, a team of six men were already there waiting for us.

"Mr. Arias, how do you want to go about this?" asked one of the men.

"We need to know how many men are guarding my family," I answered.

I had one of my men play a room service attendant and head upstairs. He said that there was only one man guarding the door but was unsure of how many could be inside.

"Juancho, this is only an assumption," Don Pacho advised. "But if it's the same number of men that picked us up in Puerto Rico, then there should only be two left."

He was right; it was twelve men that apprehended us outside of the clinic. The last guy I killed didn't even try to call for backup so we could only be dealing with two more. Due to the circumstances I didn't want to just bust in there and risk my family's safety even more. In addition to that, my family had already gone through too much in the last 12 hours so adding more men with guns wasn't going to help.

In a matter of minutes we had a young room service attendant help us out. I gave him a thousand dollars to explain the layout of the suite where Brooke and my boys were. He said that there was a master bedroom on one end of the suite with two smaller bedrooms right across. If, but only if they were being kept in one of these rooms would we use force to overtake these men.

We would have the boy take a courtesy order of chocolate fondue up there to survey the suite. He would then pretend that he had forgotten the fruit so he could come back to us and report on how many men there were and their specific locations inside the suite. After a few minutes he came back with good news; he told us that there were only two men. The last two Russians to add to my death tally. He had not seen anyone else in the suite; however, one of the two men seemed to be guarding one of the smaller rooms. That was good enough for me to move in.

I wanted to be the first person that the boys saw so I would be going up there alone at first; my men would just follow my lead. I had the same room service kid get me an outfit including a hat. We both made our way up to the suite and I could feel my blood starting to boil as we walked up to the first guy guarding the door.

"Woah, just you," he said pointing at my new young friend.

"I'm new here," I replied. "He's training me so I need to go in with him."

He extended his hand and took my nametag off.

"Your name is Sally?" He asked with a smirk as he showed me the name on the tag.

I looked back at him and before he could pull out his gun I had him on the floor with my gun to his head.

"You know something," I whispered. "I've already killed 10 of you today and I don't mind getting to twelve before the end of the night."

"Get up, play it cool and take us in," I ordered him. "If you don't do what I say you'll spit out a bullet with your name on it."

I handed the other gun to my improvised assistant who was completely speechless and asked him to hide it inside the food tray.

As we slowly made our way in I quickly looked around and there was no sign of Brooke or the boys. Suddenly my Russian man-shield shouted something in Russian, which made me react by knocking him out cold and quickly putting a bullet to the other guy's head. One thing for sure is that all these tense moments have dramatically improved my shooting accuracy ten times faster than at the gun range. The body had barely hit the ground when my men were already in the suite with me. I had them take the dead body out of the room and cover the blood splatter so the boys and Brooke wouldn't see it.

Lastly, before I walked in the bedroom where my family had been captive the whole of today, I decided to take the sole survivor of this Russian-mafia-boy-band-clan out to the balcony. We closed the door to keep the privacy and had him awaken. Once awake I told him that I was debating between two things. I could let him live and he could take a message to his pathetic mafia clan to never mess with me ever again. If they chose not to follow my advice then I would hunt every single one of them down along with their families. I would kill their wives, their children, their grandparents and if their grandparents were already dead, then I would dig them up and kill them again.

"However, my second choice also gets the message across, which is" I explained as I put a napkin with a short note for my Russian friends in one of his pockets.

"That you don't have to be alive for the note to get there." I added as I threw him over the railing.

I finally was able to be reunited with the loves of my life. Brooke's eyes appeared to be completely cried out. Christian David didn't seem to know what was going on and was fine. Rocky was crying being completely out of his element and most likely hungry. It had been an exceptionally rough day for everyone.

We walked out of the hotel, drove all the way home, put the boys to bed and Brooke remained silent. Something I couldn't get out of my mind was the way Brooke looked at me when I went in the hotel room; it was fear, as if she didn't recognize me. I admit that I might have changed in some ways recently but I'm still the same person. As I've said time and time again; all of this is for the safety and well-being of my family.

"Do you want to talk princess?" I asked Brooke as I changed for bed.

"Not right now," She answered. "I think you should sleep in one of the other bedrooms tonight."

"I want to be alone tonight so I can think things through," She added as she turned off her lamp leaving me in the dark.

"Ok, I love you," I replied with no reply back. "Have a good night."

I don't blame her for feeling this way; our new lives in Miami have been completely saturated with ups and downs in every aspect of our lives. I'd like to think that the ups have been more prevalent than the other way around. I believe that in order to achieve certain things in life you have to be willing to make sacrifices here and there. I remember the quote Don Pacho used the first time he brought me to this house.

'I have discovered in life that there are ways of getting anywhere you want to go, IF you really want to go'.

How true that is.

In a way, that Langston Hughes quote paved the way for me in building the wealth that my family gets to enjoy today and the power that I now have. Once Don Pacho is completely out of the picture, we can be truly happy.

SUNDAY JULY 3ʳᵈ, 2016

I had my driver take me to the airport to pick up the Tumbler. I drove back home where Brooke and the kids were getting ready for the day. I joined them at the dinner table and had a colorful conversation with Christian David about the mean man in the hotel. He tried explaining to me that this man screamed a lot and that he was a bad guy. He must be talking about the guy that I put a bullet into and not the one that I threw from the balcony 15 stories up.

"Juan, can you make sure to be home at 5 p.m. today?" Brooke asked as she had me help put the boys in her car.

"Yes I can," I answered. "You have something planned?"

"No, I want to talk," she replied as she buckled in.

As my family drove off I realized that it was Sunday, where was Brooke going? I pulled out my phone to call her but it went straight to voicemail; I texted but with no immediate response. I had an odd feeling so I ran upstairs and to my surprise there was no luggage in the storage room where we kept it. Had she taken the kids and left me? I tried calling again and again but the only response I had a few hours later was that she'd be home at 5 p.m. to talk.

I had the whole day to myself to think about the current situation. My mind kept going back to Don Pacho's quote, "*I have discovered in life that there are ways of getting anywhere you want to go, IF you really want to go'*.

I guess the question I should be making myself is where do I want to go? Wherever that is, I can't see myself without Brooke and the boys.

I couldn't get myself up to do anything for the rest of the day; waiting for 5 p.m. was killing me. At one point I tried to distract myself watching TV and the only thing that worked momentarily was a teaser for tonight's news.

'Join us tonight at 10 for a live interview with Police Captain, Christian Knudsen, with the Miami police department - authorities are investigating a drug related murder/ suicide at a luxury hotel in downtown Miami."

My men must have done a great job cleaning up the suite if the police are classifying this as a possible murder/suicide. It would be interesting to hear what theory they come up with about last night. I think a more interesting news headline would read more like this:

'Local businessman kills a dozen members of the Russian mafia, saves his family and is home in time for his kids' bed time.'

At exactly 5 I heard the garage door open and my pulse immediately picked up.

"How are you Brooke?" I asked timidly, "Where are the boys?"

"Let's sit Juan," she said. "The boys are with a friend, they're fine."

"I thought that it would be better to talk without any interruptions," she added while taking a seat across from me on the love couch.

"Let me talk first and then you will have your turn," Brooke proposed. "I hope that's ok with you."

After a couple of deep breaths with her eyes closed she cleared her throat and began.

"I want to start at the end first and work myself back," she explained. "I want to file for divorce."

"Juan, I'm sure you knew this was coming after you decided to lie to me," she added. "You promised me that you would talk with your boss and be done with him; that didn't happen."

"Or in other words, you didn't want that to happen," she continued.

"Despite knowing very well that you wouldn't come through, on multiple occasions you reassured me that you were only going to do the 60 pick-ups and be done. You have made some really poor decisions that have changed you dramatically within the last year. I don't even want to know what you did with the two men that kidnapped us. I honestly believe that you're no longer able to tell between what is right and wrong. You have continued to lie to yourself and in a way, convinced yourself that your decisions have always been with your family in mind; you were wrong. You have single handedly placed us, and yourself in dangerous situations. I know that you've kept me in the dark on many things. Like I said to you before, I did not marry a criminal, nor will I continue to be married to one. I need to do what is best for my boys; they need good examples in their lives, which you're not. The best thing at this time is to go our separate ways. You've clearly picked money over us so I'll begin the paperwork on Tuesday. I thought that the least I could do was to let you know."

It killed me to see Brooke like this; I am to blame for all of this. As she wiped the tears off with a tissue I remained in silence trying to figure out how to give my side of the story and not sound crazy.

"That's your reaction," Brooke asked. "I just said I wanted to divorce you and you don't show any type of emotion?"

"Brooke, I'm sorry I'm not showing any emotion," I said. "But this does kill me; especially seeing and hearing the pain I've caused you."

"Where I disagree with you is that I have had my family's best interests in mind," I added as I stood up and sat next to her.

"However, things are simply more complicated than you think," I continued.

"Then tell me!" She snapped back.

"I can't just tell you," I answered as I walked over to the kitchen looking for a piece of paper.

I wrote that our conversation was being listened to and I couldn't simply say everything that I wanted to say. I added that I had found out that Don Pacho was in reality Pablo Escobar and that he had been in hiding for the last two decades. He knew that I knew and had threatened not just us but our whole extended families. I even told her that I had been planning to kill him for some time now but everything had fallen apart; in the process Bruce was killed and my family got kidnapped. I told her to not say anything about this to anyone and to follow her plan on filing for divorce on Tuesday since everything is closed for the 4th of July. In conclusion I told her to get some cash and jump in a plane to Utah as soon as she could. She could stay with my in-laws while I had some time alone to get things taken care of between Don Pacho and myself.

"Brooke, I love you and I'm sorry for everything," I said as I gave her the note. "At this point I do think that it's best if we get a divorce."

Seeing the fear in Brooke's eyes was not easy; we hugged in silence and just like that Brooke was out the door.

Before heading upstairs I decided to get a snack while I turned on the TV to catch the news story about the "murder/suicide". I was surprised to see the same room service kid that helped us out being interviewed and giving his account of what he saw. The kid was creative and he came up with a story on his own that only reinforced the possibility of a murder/suicide; that's the kind of man that I need on my team.

With the lights off, it was time to begin rethinking my approach to the Don Pacho problem. This week would be a defining moment in my life and I couldn't afford failure. The Puerto Rico incident definitely was out of my control, which reminds me that I need to get in contact with the ladies. They must be freaking out about what went down, my whereabouts and the bad publicity on opening day to say the least. The Russians had destroyed my phone so I would have to get a new one first thing in the morning; I hope they're open be Independence Day and all. I can only imagine the anxiety from my parents hearing about what happened in San Juan and not hearing from me. After an hour of my mind going all over the place running different possible scenarios, I was finally able to calm my mind down and tune out the outside fireworks in preparation for the holiday tomorrow.

MONDAY JULY 4TH, 2016

Early morning Monday I drove to CocoWalk to get a new phone. I wasn't surprised to see a few dozen missed calls, texts, WhatsApp and Facebook messages. I took a seat on a bench in the main area and started with voicemails. The level of urgency from the ladies escalated quickly with every message that they left me. I decided to call them first and rid them of any worry; if possible, about the 'misunderstanding' with the DEA and the carnage left by the Russians that kidnapped me. It was definitely a stretch but what else could I say?

I continued with the voicemails and my parents' anxiety escalated much quicker. Not only did I not answer the phone during the whole thing, but they also couldn't get ahold of Brooke after she didn't call or text back once they touched down in Miami. Before I called my parents I listened to a few more voicemails from an unknown number; it was the exotic car rental company in Puerto Rico. They were livid, I had missed the deadline to return the Bentley and I'm sure the condition of the car did not go down so well with them. They wanted me to pay for the car. I called to tell them that instead of billing me for the repair that I would simply buy the exact same car; they asked for a 220 thousand dollar check instead.

I finally got on the phone with my parents; that went on for 2 hours. It was mainly my dad yelling at me demanding to know what I was involved in. Several times he mentioned how he knew that nothing good could ever come from my association with Don Pacho. I kept the information as vague as possible for obvious reasons trying to play down the severity of the whole thing.

"Juan Camilo," yelled my dad. "Please have some respect for us and don't treat us as if we are stupid."

"The DEA was involved AND you were kidnapped!" he added.

"People died outside of your clinic because of a shootout between drug lords," he continued without letting me get a word in for my own defense.

"Dad, I need to go right now," I said, "I'm fine, I'll call you later so we can continue our conversation."

It was a little rude from me but it was the only way to get them off the phone.

I decided to check all the texts and messages before listening to the last voicemail; nothing new from what I had already resolved or in process of resolving. I played the last voicemail; it was from an unknown number. The girl on the phone said that she was a friend of Brooke and that she had our boys. She said that Brooke had not returned last night from meeting with me. Brooke's phone had also been destroyed by the Russians so there was no way to get ahold of her. I didn't listen to the whole message but immediately called the friend and got her voicemail. As soon as I got in the Tumbler a phone call came in.

"Hello, this is Juan," I answered and asked her where she was located before she could even get a word in.

Luckily she lived in Coral Gables so I made it to her place in a matter of minutes. On my way there I stopped at a Target and bought a couple of car seats for the boys. Inside the apartment complex I parked as fast as I could and ran up three flights of stairs to the girl's apartment where Christian David was playing with her kids. I picked up my little Rocky from his Pack-and-Play and kissed him.

"I'm sorry; I never got your name," I smiled trying to seem calm.

"It's Melissa," she answered. "We met once before, I teach at the studio as well."

"Is Brooke ok?" she asked in an inquisitive and suspicious way.

Maybe she was thinking that I had to do something with her missing.

"She was a little upset after we spoke last night," I replied, "But nothing out of the ordinary."

"I'm sure she's fine," I continued. "She's done this before; she spent a night in a hotel once and left me with the kids."

I thanked her for her help, picked up our things and was out the door with the boys. In the car I began to feel true desperation. Where would she be? She had never done anything like that no matter the amount of stress or current circumstances.

"Where is mommy?" asked Christian David.

"I think she is at work," I answered as we headed to the studio.

"Mommy is dancing?" he continued.

"Yeah, we'll see her in a few minutes," I replied trying to avoid darker scenarios from entering my mind.

The studio's parking lot was empty. I was growing more worried as each minute passed by. I then remembered an app that I had installed in my old phone that allowed the user to connect up to three valuables such as cars, boats, jewelry and other priced possessions. The app would track the whereabouts of each of these things using GPS. I opened the app and clicked on Brooke's car; the other two items I had connected were my truck and Brooke's new set of earrings. The app showed that her SUV was at the airport.

Brooke's Mercedes was parked where Don Pacho and I usually parked when we left on business trips. I pulled up to the SUV and used the spare key that I had; the entire luggage was still in the back, untouched. More unwanted scenarios ran through my mind. I opened the driver's side door and my heart dropped. There it was; the note that I had given Brooke the night before on the driver's seat. Next to it was Brooke's wedding ring with a rolled up note in it.

'Juancho, after the hotel I was given very sad news about you my friend, I was informed of your recent association with Mr. Bruce Haight in the planning of my death using Botox. Let me be the first to tell you that I'm very impressed with your ingenuity and creativity, but as you can see, it doesn't go well with me. I hate to say it but reading the note you gave your wife took me over the edge and now I will be teaching you a lesson; a lesson that you will wish you never had to learn. Just like planning my death caused the death of Mr. Haight, Brooke will now have to pay a price as well; a price for your poor decision making. Don't worry; I won't be killing her- that would be letting you get off too easy.'

My worst nightmare was unfolding before me; Brooke had been taken by a monster that disregarded the value of a human life. He wouldn't think twice about hurting her to prove a point.

I picked up Brooke's ring and then it dawned on me; she was wearing the earrings last night. I opened the app again and clicked on the earrings; they were in Park City in La Catedral.

I called my pilot and told him that I needed to fly to Utah right away. He said that Don Pacho had given the pilots the 4th of July off and he was currently with his family. I replied that I would give him $100 thousand in cash if he flew me there right now; he was here ready for takeoff within the hour.

During the flight I called my parents to tell them that we were on our way to Utah. I asked them if they could watch the boys for a bit while Brooke and I took care of some business. Once we touched down at Salt Lake International I had to get a rental SUV since Don Pacho's driver was most likely up there with him right now. I dropped off the boys at my parents' house and made up some excuse as to why Brooke was not in the car with us. I spent a good amount of time kissing each of my boys in case this was the last time I saw them; one of the worst feelings I've had in my life.

"Mijo, be safe and remember who you are," said my worried mother sensing that something was off.

"You have two little guys waiting for you here," My dad added.

The harsh reality is that I really don't know what to expect.

The walk down the driveway felt like a mile as I waved back to my boys. Back in the SUV I wiped my tears off with one hand and with the other I prepped the only two weapons I had with me; a hand gun with a couple of magazines and the M16 that was almost out.

As I left my parents' neighborhood an eerie feeling crept in; loneliness mixed with hopelessness. As I tried to get my thoughts straight and tried to focus on what I was embarking myself into, I heard the same calming voice from before.

"Michael."

Wherever this voice came from, it had helped me already so in no way was I going to ignore it; not now.

"Michael."

Michael, my cousin Michael; he's a cop and the last thing I heard about him is that he is part of the SWAT team for the Salt Lake City police department. I called him and luckily he hadn't changed numbers; it was also his day off. I told him that I was in town just for tonight and I really needed to talk to him. He must have heard the urgency in my voice so he had me swing by his home in Sandy on my way up to Park City. At his place I decided that this wasn't the time to be secretive about what was really going on so I told him a slightly watered down version about the danger that Brooke and our family was facing. I didn't really have to say what kind of industry I was involved in but he knew. Without too many questions he had me follow him to his garage. He opened the back of his suburban and started prepping a couple of guns including a large one that was partially covered with a blanket.

"If what you're telling me is accurate," he said as he slipped on his bulletproof vest. "Then it wouldn't hurt us taking this as added insurance."

"It's the sniper rifle that I used when I was in Iraq," he added.

On the way up to the house I tried to explain where the house was located. He asked me about the terrain and all I could say was that it was on a hill overseeing Jordanelle Reservoir on one end and Park City Main Street on the other.

"Where on the hill is this house?" he asked.

"Tell me if he has neighbors - how close are the houses - are there any houses at a higher elevation than his – that sort of things," he added.

PARK CITY, UT

After going through all the information that I could recollect from my only time up there, we finally made it up to the property right after sunset.

With my cousin I would have a better fighting chance of getting Brooke out of this hell. He gave me an earpiece so he could communicate with me and be my eyes from up above; it was only one-way communication so I wouldn't be able to speak to him. He dropped me off about a block down from the house and he continued on and parked at the highest point he could find. After a couple of minutes he told me to make my way up the hill towards the house.

The whole street was abnormally quiet and dark, especially for a 4th of July. Then again, most of these homes are vacation homes for the elite so they're most likely empty during this time of the year. Once I made it to the gate I was given the green light to jump the fence. The black Escalade from my first time up here was parked out front with no driver. As I got closer to the main door I was told to stop and hide; three black cars were approaching.

"I'm counting six men; four are heading inside," Michael whispered into my ear. "The two outside are armed."

They were speaking German and one of the voices sounded very familiar. I wasn't able to catch a glimpse through the bushes but it sounded like Gus from the meeting in Germany.

Why was he here?

Then it hit me; the horrifying truth. The only reason why Don Pacho won't kill Brooke is because by so doing it would be letting me off too easy according to him. A more horrifying and severe punishment would be to know that she's alive but a slave; a sex slave. He was going to sell her as a sex slave. The simple thought of that happening brought tears to my eyes and made me shake in anger.

I needed to get inside now.

I stood up holding the M16 above my head and began walking towards them.

"Juan, what are you doing!?" yelled Michael into my ear.

"Excuse me Gentlemen," I said hoping that Michael had my back. "I need to get inside right now."

As one of the two men approached me to take my weapon I reacted fast just as I saw his eyes shift to the M16; I quickly reached for the handgun on my back and was able to get a clean headshot. Almost simultaneously I turned the gun to the other guy when I saw him drop with a shot to the back of the head from my cousin's rifle. Man, am I glad I called that guy.

"I've got your back primo," Michael said as I picked up the M16 and made my way in the house.

"Be safe," he added.

As I stepped in and walked past the foyer I began to hear distant laughter coming from the downstairs area. I looked at the reflection on the large windows by the staircase and could see that they were in the underground pool area. As I took each step slowly I kept my eyes on the reflection. I still couldn't see Brooke. I counted one, two, three men –

wait, I stopped walking, where's the fourth one? I hadn't finished that thought when I felt a gun to the back of my head.

"I need you to give me your weapon Mr. Arias," the fourth man said in a German/Spanish accent. "Now move."

"Juancho, I'm so glad you were able to make it," Don Pacho said as I was brought to my knees.

"Where's Brooke you bastard," I yelled as I looked around.

"How did he get past my two men outside?" Gus asked.

"Oh Gus, you don't know Juancho that well; just two men will never be able to contain him," Don Pacho replied. "He can be a beast under the right circumstances; he just needs a little nudge once in a while."

"Where's my wife?" I yelled again.

"Juancho, first of all – bring it down a notch," he said. "No need to yell; we're not deaf."

"She's fine; a little sore, but she's ok," he added as he signaled his driver to bring her out.

"She's beautiful," Gus said as Brooke was brought out of the wine cellar. "I'll definitely taker her."

"Excuse me, we haven't talked price yet," the other German said. "Let's not get ahead of ourselves."

My heart sank as I saw how horrible she was; they had her wearing only lingerie, her mouth was covered with duct tape and her hands tied in front of her with a zip tie. As she was thrown to me I tried to stand up to get a towel from a nearby pool chair but I was pushed backed down.

"Let me get a towel so I can at least cover her," I said.

"Brooke, I am so sorry for getting you in all of this," I whispered into her ear as I hugged her and cried with her. I carefully took off the duct tape and wiped the tears with the towel.

"So Don Pacho," Gus chuckled. "How was she?"

"She was definitely one of the best in my opinion," he answered and took a puff from his cigar.

I looked at both of these animals trying to understand what they were referring to as Brooke held me tighter and began to be inconsolable.

"He raped me Juan," she could barely complete her sentence.

"Actually three times to be exact," he replied. "I've had my eye on her for a while now."

"I had to get a test drive in if I was to know how much she's worth," he added.

I wanted to jump and break his neck but I continued to hold Brooke tightly in my arms.

"I'm going to enjoy killing you," I said calmly. "I'm going to finish what the DEA and the government couldn't do two decades ago."

"Couldn't or wouldn't?" he laughed.

"Juancho, you surprise me," he continued. "I thought that by now you wouldn't ask stupid questions or make comments like that."

"Listen to me, this is the last time that I'll say this to you," he explained. "Everything, absolutely everything in this world has a price."

"Whether it's a cop, a politician, the Pope or even my friend George Bush senior," he added, "They all have a price."

"So was it a body double that they shot on that roof top in Medellin twenty-three years ago?" I asked as I tried coming up with a way to get us out of this.

"Wouldn't you want to know my friend," he replied. "The only thing I'll say about it is that the whole thing was worthy of an Oscar in Hollywood."

"Juancho, that was a perfect example of how creativity and team work can rule supreme in a getaway situation," he added as he drew his gun and walked over to me.

"Stand him up," he ordered.

As he rested the gun on my forehead his driver pointed out that I had an earpiece.

"What the hell is this?" Don Pacho yelled as he took it out of my ear. "Who is with you?"

I immediately heard glass shattering and a couple of smoke canisters going off. As the room quickly filled up with smoke I was able to knock the gun off of Don Pacho's hand knocking him and his driver down at the same time. I quickly jumped on top of Brooke to protect her as a wave of bullets began to fly every direction. After a good sixty seconds everything went silent. Once the smoke cleared I opened my eyes and noticed that Don Pacho was still down; he had been accidentally shot in the chest by one of his own men.

I got up to pick up his gun just as my cousin Michael said the worst thing I could've heard at that moment.

"Primo, Brooke was hit!" he yelled.

To my horror she was face down in a pool of her own blood.

"Brooke!" I threw myself down and turned her around. She was still alive but barely.

"Brooke, look at me – can you open your eyes for me please princess?" I asked frantically as I caressed her face; she had been shot in the neck and was losing blood quickly.

"Juan, you're hit too," Michael said pointing at my shoulder.

"Please don't leave me Brooke," I sobbed uncontrollably as I tried to apply pressure with the towel. "The boys and I need you with us."

She opened her tearful eyes for a moment, opened her mouth and whispered something under her breath; I leaned in.

"Juan, you killed me," she whispered again as I felt her leave me.

As I held Brooke's lifeless body in my arms I cried as I never have before. Brooke was right, I had killed her; I had brought all of this craziness to my family and now Brooke was gone.

"I'm so sorry primo," Michael said quietly as he rested his hand on my shoulder.

"What do you want to do with him?" he asked referring to Don Pacho who was inching himself towards the stairs. He had also been shot in one of his legs and was leaving a trail of blood as he dragged himself across the room.

As my focus shifted to Pablo I immediately stopped crying; I stood up and picked up the handgun I had taken from him. As I slowly walked over to him, he turned around in silence and rested himself on the stairs. We both looked at each other without a word spoken. He wasn't begging for his life; he knew that it would be pointless. As I raised the gun and held it to his head I found myself thinking that he didn't deserve to die like this.

"No, not like this," I whispered just loud enough for him to hear.

"Aahhh..." he yelled in excruciating pain as I shot both of his knees.

Without a word I went up the stairs and down the hall to his bedroom. Just like before I entered his walk-in closet, put in the password and the safe opened up revealing the golden gun, cash and what I was here for; the ancient Samurai sword. As I made my way down the hall I dragged the blade along the expensive rugs splitting them in half.

He was still at the bottom of the stairs waiting for me.

I knelt down in front of him and stared into his eyes; surprisingly, I couldn't see any sign of fear - the fear of death.

"Juancho, I taught you well," he chuckled looking at the sword and struggled for air.

"I saw the potential in you from the moment I first met you," he continued. "I waited two whole decades for someone I could trust; little did I know that I would find that person in one of my car washes."

"It's ironic that my life ends in your hands," he added, "No one could bring me down - not the DEA, the FBI, the CIA, Los PEPES, the Colombian or American governments; it would eventually be a part-time carwash supervisor."

After a few moments of silence I realized that I had nothing else to say to this parasite so I stood up as he uttered his last words.

"You will never be able to leave this world behind; power will become your oxygen," he concluded just as I lifted the sword above his head and with one swing I ended the life of the man who took everything from me.

AUGUST 20TH, 2024 – MIAMI, FL

Eight long years have gone by since that horrible night in July when Brooke was taken from us. Life truly hasn't been the same without her here. She was the love of my life in every sense of the word; she was my life. I like to remind myself that she is still here in a way; I've been lucky to see Christian David and Rocky grow into strong, healthy and smart young men. Christian David has turned into a handsome 12-year-old ladies' man; just like his old man at that age. Rocky is a vibrant 8-year-old that doesn't take crap from anyone; I've been called to school several times because of fighting. I think Brooke's absence has hit him the most even though he doesn't remember her at all.

In the days following that night we buried Brooke in the same cemetery where her grandma was buried in Draper. My cousin Michael took care of everything about that dreadful night and to this day I'm not sure what he said happened there. I'd be curious to hear what his explanation was for the beheading of Pablo.

With Brooke's absence my parents offered to move to Florida to help me raise the boys; they've been a tremendous help these past few years. Before Brooke's death we had discussed leaving Miami for good and retiring to Utah; however, with the business empire I built it was definitely more convenient to remain put here. We've made several trips back to Utah to check up on our business ventures and visit Brooke's parents; they enjoy having the boys there. I know they blame me for their daughter's death but I can't hold that against them; they're more than right. I can also sense the same thing with my parents but their love for their grandsons keeps them here. I never remarried; dating yes but I haven't found anyone that can measure up to Brooke. She was definitely one of a kind; I miss her.

I decided to sell our Coral Gables mansion since every corner of that house reminded me of Brooke. It was also an opportunity to build a custom home now that my parents were going to live with us. I decided to tear down Palazzo Napoli and build a 23,000 square foot French Chateau mansion; I named it Le Rêve.

Two months after the death of Pablo I was contacted by his legal team at my office. They brought up an interesting bit of information that caught me by surprise; six months prior to his death he had completed all the legalities and paperwork necessary to make me the sole recipient of everything he owned after he passed away - The mansions, the cars, the business ventures, the 100+ billion dollar fortune. In reality he wasn't prepping me to be only his right hand man; No, he saw me as the person that would become his eventual successor.

Despite the several life-changing decisions that I've had to make along the way in the past year, it still amazes me that there is always something bigger and more extreme that comes along. I still remember putting the boys to bed that night contemplating whether I really had it in me to become the next head of this global cartel; most importantly, the successor of Pablo Escobar. I had learned everything there was to learn about this global organization from the founder and creator himself. If I was going to take this on then I did not want to be seen simply as the next

Escobar; I would become something bigger.

I would be in charge of creating my own legend.

BASE - EMPIRE

As we walked inside a large conference room inside The Brooke Hotel &

Resort in Monaco; the room with over 200 wealthy and powerful men

stood up immediately as Juan made his way towards the front of the

room. The respect that all members of our organization have for Juan still

astonishes me even after the eight years that I've been working for him.

I take my seat in the back as the person in charge of all audio/visual

equipment since Juan doesn't want any hotel staff to be present at these

meetings. Shortly after the first meeting a few years back some

information fell into the wrong hands so we had to change the format for

the following years. This makes it the fourth year that we've been hosting these types of meetings; they're held semi-annually - April and October. Juan says that the only way that this global organization can work in harmony is to meet in person more than one time per year; it minimizes room for error and misunderstandings. He says that this is the main reason why he built this resort; for these meetings while putting a façade as a major Mediterranean destination.

I quickly sync up the tablet that Juan will be using to the room's main A/V system and run it up to him; He prefers using slideshows and spreadsheets to get the point across. The meetings always go for two hours to the dot with a quick 15-minute bathroom break. My job is to supervise and assist in case there are any technical issues during the presentation; nothing ever happens anyways.

In the meantime, let me introduce myself. My name is Nic with no K; Nic is short for Nicolas Illaramendi. I was born and raised in Miami to a Spanish father and a Colombian mother. My parents died shortly after I was born in a car accident caused by a drunk driver; one of the main reasons why I don't drink. I have two siblings; an older sister who is married and lives in my dad's hometown of Valladolid, Spain. The city is about an hour drive north from Madrid. My other sibling is a younger sister that lives in Miami with my aunt and her family; I moved them out to my house in Coconut Grove a year after I began working for Juan. Cristina is 17 years old and will be graduating from Ransom Everglades School next year; I wanted to make sure that she got the best education possible since I can afford it.

I'm turning 26 years old next month, I'm single; I have a net worth of $33 million and an annual salary of $5 million. I live a pretty good life but never forgetting about serving my own family and other less fortunate individuals in the community.

One of the many things that I've learned from working with such a powerful and successful individual like Juan is that it's more important to give than to receive. Juan volunteers several times per month at different locations in the greater Miami area and simply serves people. Everyone in the company is required to serve in the community at least twice per month; it's literally in all the job descriptions. I speak twice a month at various high schools around Miami about my success and how I continue to value education even after making my millions.

I was only 17 years old when I met Juan; I was working in room service at the JW Marriott when he pulled me to the side and had me help him that one night in 2016. I made $1,000 dollars that night; more than I made in a whole month. A few weeks later Juan came in the hotel asking for me with a job offer that would change my whole life. To this day he tells me that he knew he wanted me in his team when he saw me come on TV and according to him - I displayed a coolness and maturity when I was interviewed about the events of that night. It has been eight years since that day and I will never regret dropping everything for a spot in Juan's team.

I graduated high school that following summer because Juan said that I had to; I would've dropped out, I was already making 6-figures by then. However, Juan took a real and deep interest in my education and I will eternally thank him for that; I got my undergraduate degree in business followed by an MBA. Now I can see how important that was for me as I've advanced in responsibility within the company but also in the organization. I doubt I would be making $5 million per year or have a tenth of the net worth I enjoy today if I had dropped out of high school.

"Gentlemen, this is the reason why in the last five years," explained Juan as he moved on to the next slide, "We have completely taken over two of the biggest markets in the world."

The markets that Juan was referring to were the Indian and Chinese markets; major achievements for our organization. I'm proud to say that I had a good size part in the success of obtaining the China market. Shortly after finishing my MBA, Juan assigned me to oversee important portions of the strategy to take full control of said market from its previous heads. It took a few years longer than expected but with persistence and a few bullets - we got the job done. I'm convinced that this is why I've ascended quickly up the 'corporate' ladder; I never gave up and in a way I always saw each failure as an opportunity in disguise.

I won't deny the fact that as time has passed by and the responsibility has dramatically increased; my levels of stress and anxiety attacks have also grown. I've always wanted to go above and beyond for Juan; in a way – prove my worth to him. I do however work for the best boss that anyone could ever work for; in addition to mentoring me all these years, he also encouraged me to find a hobby. Being a soccer player he encouraged me to pick it up as my sport; he even invited me to join one of his teams. On multiple occasions over the years he has reminded me that my Spanish and Colombian ancestors would be appalled at the fact that I don't like soccer.

I do play basketball regularly but where I found my sweet spot is in business. The fact that I didn't have to struggle too much to have the capital to start several businesses has been a stress reliever on its own. Although I have ventured in many different industries my baby from the beginning has been BASE Empire. The idea to start a lifestyle-clothing brand for entrepreneurs came to me in the thick of obtaining the Chinese drug empire. As I always say – every failure is an opportunity in disguise - became a motivator to motivate others as well.

The way I see it is that it doesn't matter if you're a salesman for a cell phone company, a real estate agent, a small business owner or someone in my industry; what you define as success will only come if you want it to and if you're willing to do everything that is necessary to achieve it.

The reason behind naming it BASE Empire originated from the first few years of working for Juan. As he became the head of our organization, he spent the first few years making a mantra for the organization. He called it 'having your BASE at all times' – it was an acronym for Believe, Act, Sell and Endure. He swore by this in business and believed that it could be applied to becoming lasting leaders in the drug world. The decision to add the word "Empire" to my brand also came from Juan; he said that it was imperative for me to build a solid financial empire for my family and descendants.

"Did it flow?" asked Juan about the presentation as he handed me the tablet.

"Also, make sure that the jet is all set and ready to go as soon as we get to the airport," he continued. "I want to be in the air within the hour."

"Yes and yes," I replied as I turned it off and picked up the last few things. "Our driver should already be outside waiting for us."

As we made our way through the lobby Juan stopped by the center grand piano to listen to a voicemail.

"Rocky got in a fight again," Juan sighed. "I feel so sorry for my little guy."

We were just about to get in the car when we began to hear some commotion behind us. A couple of men were helping one of our hotel guests out the door who appeared to be going into labor. As one of the men attempted to get a taxi Juan called out to them and told them to take our car. After a few seconds of convincing they accepted.

"Good luck with the delivery." Shouted Juan as he closed the door and our driver took off through the busy Monaco traffic.

"Bad traffic day to be having a baby," he chuckled as a call came in.

I could still see the car weaving through the sea of cars; it was going to be bumper to bumper all the way to the hospital.

"Who's this!?" Juan yelled just as I saw our car with the pregnant woman explode knocking us and everyone around to the ground.

The air was quickly filled with car alarms, people screaming and sirens – I was able to ask everyone if they were okay. As I leaned over to help Juan up I was caught off guard by the expression on his face and by the first words out of his mouth.

"We are at war."

.

Made in the USA
Las Vegas, NV
31 January 2023

66504656R00203